INTRODUCING THEORY

FRAMING

AND THE VISUAL

ART

MICHAEL CARTER

---

transvisual studies

transvisual studies

Other titles in the Transvisual Studies series:
Old Worlds New Visions   Tony Fry
Illusions of Identity: the art of nation   Anne-Marie Willis

INTRODUCING THEORY

FRAMING

AND THE VISUAL IMAGE

ART

MICHAEL CARTER

transvisual studies

Hale & Iremonger

For my grandfather Cyril Carter.
A remarkable man in so many ways.

Typeset, printed & bound by
Southwood Press Pty Limited
80–92 Chapel Street, Marrickville, NSW

For the publisher
Hale & Iremonger Pty Limited
GPO Box 2552, Sydney, NSW

National Library of Australia Cataloguing-in-publication entry

Carter, Michael, 1944–   .
    Framing art: introducing theory and the visual image.

    Includes index.
    ISBN 0 86806 355 X (pbk).

    1. Art — Philosophy. 2. Art — History. 3. Visual
perception. I. Title. (Series: Transvisual studies).

701

Contents

8

9

Preface

The impulse to write the book you are about to read was provided by a student. After a particularly gruelling session I was asked whether there was a simple introductory text that she could consult. When I replied that no such work existed, she retorted 'Then write one!' Before this I had resisted the idea and I continued to be rather cold towards such a task for reasons that I now regard as residual Romanticism on my part. One of the pleasures of teaching an introductory course in Art History was precisely its uncodified state. It was, and still is, a 'fluid' discipline, remarkably dependent upon the particular intellectual equipment of the personnel teaching it. The years passed and I became increasingly dissatisfied with this state of affairs as every year new bibliographies had to be produced, new concepts and intellectual fashions gripped the teaching body and new vocabularies swept through the art world like bushfires. But it was also clear that despite these annual re-toolings there was a persistent sediment of material and ideas that was crucial for students to become familiar with. 'Codification' was taking place whether I liked it or not.

What follows is an attempt to isolate this recurring core of ideas and make it available in a form that is understandable and yet still carries within it some of the dynamism and excitement created by an intellectual discipline undergoing a profound sea-change in all aspects of its operations.

Whenever such intellectual shifts take place there is, for a time, a gap between those working at the forefront of such changes and those whose task it is to prepare students for the more advanced work at tertiary level and beyond. The excitement of the chase, the deployment of new vocabularies and the iconoclastic impulse that is an inevitable accompaniment to such change can appear from the outside very daunting. At times it must seem as if those engaged in such activities are slightly deranged. In the daily warfare that is Art History at the moment, it is easy for teachers to forget the initial moves that propelled them out into the new territory. It is all too easy to lose sight of *why* it was felt necessary to introduce *that* particular concept at *that* particular moment; and sadly, it is easy to forget what *was* at stake in making *that* intellectual move. Theoretical and emotional amnesia can too often be a product of this drive for the new.

Perhaps the most persistent criticism levelled at the new ways of doing Art History and Visual Studies is that of jargon. Non-initiates feel that they are being hoodwinked, deceived, or simply are being excluded from a charmed circle that maintains its exclusivity not by the novelty of its findings, but by a novelty in language whose function is to reiterate the already familiar through the use of barbarous neologisms. Teaching is seen as a process of inducting the novitiate into this intellectual liturgy.

It would be naive to suppose that such anxieties could be dispelled by a declaration by me that it is not so. It is the task of this book to engage directly with such fears and hopefully demonstrate that, whilst understandable, such accusations are, at best, misguided, at worst, ideologically motivated. Very often those most vehement in their denunciations of the new ways of doing Art History are not as innocent as they like to appear. More often than not they are dissembling a disagreement with the *content* of such ideas beneath a rhetoric of plain speaking. Having said this, vocabulary and use of language is certainly the point where the tensions between the old (and not so old) and the new can be seen at their most intense. I wish to make a plea, if not for jargon, then certainly for linguistic novelty and conceptual precision and one anecdote will serve my purpose here.

For relaxation one of my favourite areas of reading is popular science, particularly astronomy and physics. I recently encountered a volume on quantum mechanics where the writer was at pains to stress that in order to grasp the major tenets of the new physics, one had to start from the fact that 'things are not as they appear', that the concepts, images, vocabulary and syntax derived from our everyday reality were inadequate when it came to describing the micro-world of particle physics. 'Inadequacy' is a mild way of putting it because at this level much of what we take as given in the realm of physical matter is contradicted by the behaviour of the micro-particles that make up the physical world of commonsense.

The comparison between quantum mechanics and Visual Arts is perhaps overly melodramatic, but it alerts us to the fact that the concepts, the vocabulary, even the grammar of our descriptive sentences is not a mere quibble or hair-splitting exercise. Might it not be the case that in order to grasp the operations of the Visual Arts we may have to put to one side the languages of commonsense — and therefore the worlds of commonsense — as well as commiting a degree of violence upon our inherited languages. Sometimes this may entail only a slight adjustment, or even something as minor as a different emphasis. At other times a wholesale re-speaking or re-writing may be required for the novel concept to emerge in its full richness. The value of any such conceptual 'smithying' is in direct relation to the extent it enables what is being studied to open up for the student. It is in its usage that an idea demonstrates its worth.

Finally I should like to make it clear that this volume is really a *user's manual* for beginners, rather than a text book. Too much is absent for it to be granted such a status. The author has said what could be said with a degree of clarity, about everything else he — wisely I think — decided to remain silent.

Michael Carter

Acknowledgements

I would like to thank all my colleagues in the Department of Fine Arts for their patience in answering my perpetual stream of queries; Terry Threadgold who listened to my doubts; Anne-Marie Willis for her editorial assistance; Diane Losche for the Abelam material; Deborah Malor and Stephen Schaeffer whose filing systems are more efficient than mine; Fay Brauer for a diagram; Nadia Pearce for the word processing; Robin Appleton for her editing; Jenni Carter for her help with the illustrations; Céline Fitzpatrick for her help with the cover; last, but certainly not least, my thanks to Tony Fry for his friendship and advice throughout the writing of this book.

Introduction

A definition of what the study of Art History consists of is fine just so long as there is general agreement upon what *Art* is and what *History* is. If there are serious difficulties about defining either word, let alone what these might add up to when they are placed together, then the assumptions upon which the discipline has rested in the past start to become very shaky. It is precisely this undermining of the foundations that has been taking place during the 1980s.

The people working within the area of Art History are fond of describing the condition of their discipline as that of crisis. If by 'crisis' we mean 'a condition in which accepted frameworks, ideas, assumptions and vocabularies no longer seem to be working', then Art History is certainly in a crisis. But it is easy to panic and see one's immediate situation as desperate. A wider view would reveal that these local quaverings are part of a much wider condition of ferment afflicting the study of the Arts, perhaps even the Humanities in general. My own feeling about these changes is that the study of the Visual Arts is growing up a little and that part of this process of growing up is to admit that there are many different ways of looking at the area termed Art, ways that cannot be easily contained within the title 'Art History'.

I want to spend the remainder of this chapter looking at just a few of the changes that are taking place and I want to do this by focusing in on the unofficial title of the discipline, Art History. I will do this by examining each element — Art and History —

separately and conclude by re-uniting the two words in the light of the arguments advanced.

Art

Looking at the *Art* component of the title Art History, we are straightaway faced with the problem that very few people working in the Fine Arts — whether as practitioners or studiers — would be prepared to put forward a definition of art that would enable us to pin it down once and for all. I should perhaps add that this is not because the discipline hasn't found one yet — there have been hundreds — nor is it due to the so-called subjective nature of the entity art and the inevitably unstable ground any such definition will find itself on. It is rather a symptom of a much wider problem which is encountered in the study of all human artifacts and behaviour, namely that the same species that is being studied is doing the studying. Inevitably, this means that any attempt to produce a definition is always going to be entangled in the lives of those trying to arrive at the definition. This does not automatically rule out the possibility of arriving at a definition, but what it does do is place rigid limits upon the nature of the understanding and knowledge that we can reasonably expect to produce. Any investigation of the Fine Arts is always going to be an amalgam of the *objective* and the *subjective* — a delicate threading together of general and particular types of understanding. We must always realise that the explanations it is able to put forward are never going to be able to attain the level of those demanded in science.

I want to elaborate this general assertion of the limits to our understanding by way of five different examples, each of which is intended to highlight that 'Art' is always a flexible and shifting entity.

The linguistic limitation

Simply at the level of language, the word 'Art' operates in three dimensions

It is a word. That is a sound with a meaning.

It is a mental image. Something which for English speakers engenders a set of associations, some of which are personal while others will be communal.

It is a relationship. That is the word (the sound) and the associations it calls up will refer to a class of objects, for example art works.

On the basis of this it is possible to say that the word 'Art' can do two things. It can designate/point to a set of objects that it is generally agreed are art objects, but it can also designate a set of additional objects which a specific individual may regard as art objects.

If for the moment we remain with the simpler situation of general agreement between word/concept/object we can immediately destabilise these correspondences by introducing the factor of time (Fig. 1).

	1200 AD	1700 AD	1800 AD	1900 AD	Present
Word	?	Art	Art	Art	Art
Concept	?	a	b	c	d
Objects	?	A	B	C	D

Figure 1

If we begin with the top line of Figure 1, namely the historical usages of the word 'Art' in the English language, it is possible to discover that while the word 'Art' occurs regularly in the language, before the 13th century the word was not present. Does this mean that, in England, before the 13th century there were no such things as 'art objects' because the culture lacked such a word? Even when the word 'Art' begins to occur — somewhere in the 13th century — it is clear that it has a different set of associations to those current today and referred to a different set of objects. Hence we may have a linguistic continuity in that a recognisable word 'art' is in usage, but the mental associations and the objects referred to are very different. We should never assume that because there is a continuity at the first level — that of language — that there exists a complementary set of continuities at the other two levels.

This gives us a general principle, namely that the linguistic structures (vocabulary, syntax, and so on) we use in the present to designate Art should not be seen as trans-historical (applicable to all times past). Even when there appear to be similarities further investigation will reveal wide discrepancies between past and current usage.

Cultural relativism
What we noted above in relation to the passage of time applies with equal force to the usage of terms like 'Art' to different cultures. My earlier remark about the difficulties that arise from humans studying their own artifacts and behaviours is pertinent here. A term like 'Art' carries in its various meanings and associations both traces of the past ways of life of the society in which it is being used as well as influences arising from the position its current users find themselves in. For instance, within European societies Art has meant not only 'skilfully produced objects' but also the 'quality which the maker imparted to them' — *artfulness*. It also contributed to the idea of artificiality as well as the assumptions of its opposite — the natural as being morally superior to the domain of 'artifice'. Many of these usages of the word may have receded but today Art, as an idea, still resonates with many assumptions that form the basis of our way of life; the contrasts between Art and industry, Art and science, and artistic personalities versus practical ones.

It should be clear that the word 'Art' is never a straightforward way of designating a distinctive set of objects. It has been a word capable of calling up a shifting and complex set of associations. In other cultures there may not be an equivalent word for Art, for instance objects that have come to be designated as Art in our culture may be placed within the categories of religious paraphernalia, or the sacred. Even where we find a rough approximation — and there are many such cultures which recognise certain objects as carrying strong manifestations of the aesthetic — it may be that the meanings that such objects have for their users are very different from the equivalent objects in our own culture.

In the 19th century an overly confident belief in the correctness of one's own way of life lead many sensitive thinkers on art to dismiss completely the objects from other cultures.

> In Christian Europe alone pure and precious ancient art exists, for there is none in America, none in Asia, none in Africa.
>
> (John Ruskin)

Few today would subscribe to such a dismissive attitude but its opposite courts certain dangers as well. As a reaction to this earlier narrowness it is easy to make the mistake of lowering our linguistic and intellectual frameworks onto other cultures in order to claim that they have Art just like ours. This may be done with the best intentions and the result may not be all that dissimilar from the views of the 19th century. Do we not by such operations, re-make the non-European into an image of the European, by claiming that Art is a universal phenomena, something that all people in all places do?

To sensitise ourselves to the differences in significance that both objects and behaviours have for the people using the objects and performing the behaviours we must ascertain what significance the objects have for the people with that particular way of life. We can go some way to avoiding the imposition of ideas and explanations that are entwined with our ways of living.

The Modernist criticism of Art

So far I have raised the factors of time and place as limiting our definitions of 'Art'. However, if we were to decide to remain within one culture and try to restrict ourselves in terms of the time span we were studying, surely then it would be possible to agree upon something that we all recognise as Art. That would be a possibility if it were not for the peculiar nature of the time and place in which we find ourselves and from which I too am speaking. That is the 20th century and a culture which is one of the inheritors of European civilisation.

For this part of the argument I want to shift our focus onto the practitioners of Art and look particularly at the people who together produced that rather loose entity Modern Art. For the sake of brevity I take this to refer (however loosely) to those men and women, living in Europe, who towards the end of the 19th century and the beginning of the 20th set out to produce a type of Art that is regularly referred to as 'Modernist'. (I also include those artists of the 20th century who inherited the Modernist project.)

⌈ Part of the project of creating this 'New Art for a new age' was to scrutinise/criticise/demolish not just *the styles* in which Art had previously been produced, but to dismantle the grammar and syntax by and through which artists made objects which had a collective significance. What they were engaged in was a continuous attempt to re-define what Art was. ⌉

Three examples are given here to illustrate the degree to which

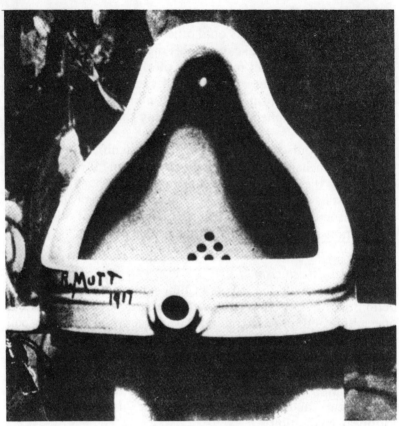

1. Marcel Duchamp: *Fountain* 1917

they searched out the basic assumptions and definitions upon which the current collective definition of Art rested.

Each of these artists, in different ways, attempted to undermine certain key elements in our definition of Art.

Marcel Duchamp (ill. 1) shifted the epicentre of Art from making an object to choosing an object and so questioned the distinction between Art and non-Art objects.

Jean Arp (ill. 2) consciously used the operations of chance to construct his image and so moved Art away from being the outcome of the work of the artist as a highly trained decision maker in the domain of the aesthetic.

Carl Andre (ill. 3) by deliberately using randomness in the work of Art mounts a criticism of the work as a site of order and structure.

2. Jean Arp: *Collage Arranged According to the Laws of Chance* 1916-17.
Torn and pasted papers, 48.6 x 34.6 cm
(Collection, Museum of Modern Art, New York)

3. Carl Andre: *Rockpile* 1968

In using such examples I wish to illustrate the fact that one of the tasks of the Modernist artist has been to re-define what Art is and thereby alter what may be thought of as Art. I suspect that many Art Historians wish that all this demolition and re-definition had never taken place. But whatever one's views, the fact that this work has come to be accepted as Art (even if it is not liked) has meant that those whose task it is to study the Fine Arts have had to incorporate such re-definitions into their own outlooks. The acceptance of this uncertainty principle as to exactly what is and is not Art is part of Fine Arts and its study.

Feminist re-definitions
If you re-examine Figure 1 on page 13, it should be clear that for each of our (arbitary) points in time the concept of Art may vary. It is also the case that each moment through time may also be *retro-active*, seeking to re-examine and even re-define the nature of the concepts that were current previous to it. So, not only will each of the present moments of 'Art' be grasped differently, its past moments will also undergo change.

This process of *retro-active re-definition* can be illustrated by examining the impact which Feminist thinking has had on both the practice and the study of the Fine Arts over the past fifteen years.

During the 1970s and 1980s much cogent criticism was directed at the Art world by the Feminist Movement. It was pointed out that women were under-represented as the makers of Art. But the criticisms went deeper and demonstrated that many of the elementary concepts about Art were influenced by the dominance of men in Art History.

Feminist critics pointed out that it was the objects made by men that were designated as Art, while those made by women were mostly relegated to the areas of Craft or work related to the home environment where women were particularly active. So we find a three part division operating
- Art
- Craft
- Domestic skills

Art History tended to be an account of Art objects (as they were defined) and therefore was overwhelmingly a history of men's activity. But what of those areas that were categorised as either craft or domestic skills such as needlework, embroidery, the organisation and building of the home environment? Some feminist Art

4. Miriam Shapiro: *Black bolero* 1980. Fabric, glitter and synthetic polymer on canvas, 182.9 x 365.8 cm (Art Gallery of New South Wales)

Historians and artists started to argue that because there were so many barriers against women entering the Arts, it was precisely in these 'lesser' areas that women's manual skills and aesthetic sensibilities could flourish to any degree. The results of such criticisms led to the emergence of two responses. Women artists began to avail themselves of the skills which had previously been categorised as non-artistic areas (*see* ill. 4). Whilst women Art Historians began to re-write the accounts of Western Art in order to draw attention to these huge areas of female activity that had previously been ignored. In other words the impact of Feminism on Art History has been retro-active and has reached back into the past of our culture in order to re-define what is and is not thought of as Art.

Contemporary Art practice
Finally there is the practice of contemporary artists to come to terms with. Many of these artists are no respecters of definitions of Art dreamed up by critics and Art Historians and are more likely to follow an idea or theme where it takes them. If this violates what is 'expected' of an artist then so much the better.

The work of a young Australian artist, Maria Kozic, will illustrate these difficulties.

The point to be made about an artist like Kozic is that her work moves across and uses a variety of media. She avails herself of paint, silkscreen, film, video, fashion and music. It can be three-dimensional or two-dimensional. She will use *combinations* of media, or mix traditional forms like painting along with newer

5. Mariä Kozic: *Godzilla* 1983 (Kind permission of the artist)

'untried' media such as video. At the level of the content of her work she takes pleasure in mixing material from high Art and mass forms and is not averse to incorporating second-hand or third-hand imagery (*see* ill. 5). What we have here is an artistic practice which is a long way from the more traditional idea of the artist as someone who operates mainly in one medium and who is a specialist in producing original and individual objects characterised by a high degree of manual dexterity, someone who is in the business of making things that are soaked with the personal signature of the artist.

When we put each of these factors together their cumulative effect upon the study of the Fine Arts has been twofold. Firstly any single definition of Art is always going to be inadequate to the current practice of Art. The Art world is so diverse and plural as to render any single definition immediately obsolete. Parallel to this, some of the factors I've touched upon – the linguistic, cultural, and Feminist revisions – are more properly seen as *internal*; factors that have tended to destabilise the traditional ways of studying Art History. When these factors are combined we find that instead of a single, unified concept of Art, Art History has had to come to terms with the fact that there are many ways of defining and doing Art. This in turn has shattered what was perhaps the most important function of the discipline in the past; to produce a unified set of values whereby the good and the worthy could be distinguished from the bad and the spurious. Today those studying the Fine Arts are much more likely to describe what they do as *explaining/explanation* than the production of a set of value judgements about particular Art works or artists.

History
If, as I argue, there has been a profound destabilisation of the idea

of Art, the other half of the term, the word 'History', has also been undergoing examination and re-formation?

The arguments about the naming of a discipline might initially appear to be petty, but these are usually symptoms of much deeper disturbances and can have direct results for students wishing to enter the discipline. The current problems around the term 'history' are responsible for the most immediate differences in the ways in which students are taught.

The problem of History can be broken down into three interconnected areas:

Problems of historical knowledge
The question of the story or narrative of History
The results of historical plurality or differential Histories

Historical knowledge

At the outset nothing would appear simpler than to define 'history'. It consists of 'everything that is past'. The task of the Art Historian then is to find out what happened in the past and 'tell it like it was'. If proper research is undertaken, if the historian is both accurate and objective, then it should be possible — given the presence of the appropriate evidence — to approximate to what really happened. As new evidence is discovered, improvements upon past accounts will be possible. Gradually our knowledge of the past should improve.

Unfortunately, very little History is like that and Art History even less so. If we take one image — say *Self-Portrait*, by Vincent van Gogh (September 1889) — we can see how inadequate such a view of Art History is.

When we are confronted with such an image what precisely is an historical explanation of it? Where do we start? None of the answers to such questions are self-evident and each involves a myriad of decisions and assumptions about what both History and explanation mean.

At the most literal of levels we might attempt an explanation of such an image by way of a description of its physical properties

its dimensions
what types of paint were used
what it is painted on
what kind of frame does it have

But such a *description* does not give an explanation. Although some of this physical description may be relevant, it is rather like trying to explain a football match in terms of the molecular composition of the players and the ball. We need to recognise that while the image in question is a physical object, it is always more than that. It is physical matter that has been shaped, and organised into a visual image. Given this, we need to have some ideas about what a visual image is. Again, there are as many ideas about this as there are images.

We might achieve more if we describe the surface organisation of the image, detailing the particular deployment of line, colour, and shape. We could talk about the nature of the brush strokes, the painting's surface patina, or how the image is internally organised (its composition). Once again, this type of description may be essential for an adequate explanation, but it too comes up against the problem that a description of the deployment of physical material upon a two-dimensional surface is insufficient in order for us to grasp what is essential about an image. It is rather like describing a brick wall by detailing each individual brick, but failing to grasp what a brick wall is, what the function of a wall might be. Other approaches to this image may be attempted. Having ascertained that it is by the individual known as Vincent Van Gogh, we could verify that it is in fact a self-portrait. The historian may then attempt an explanation in terms of Van Gogh's personality. The image then becomes an aspect of Van Gogh the man. Even here there are problems. For such an explanation to be adequate and sufficient one has to decide

what a personality is

what Van Gogh's personality was

make the assumption that Van Gogh painted the picture in such a way as to illustrate his personality

We might refuse such an approach on the grounds that it assumes too much about Art as an expressive vehicle for the artist and instead choose to remain strictly within the pictures themselves. Having verified the date in which it was painted we may set out to see how *this* particular image compares with the images the artist produced before that date and those that followed it. Historical explanation now might like to argue that the *Self-Portrait* represents the next logical step in the unfolding of Van Gogh's *style*. It might be seen as the summation of (or regression from) what had gone before and a starting-point for what was to follow. Such an explanation assumes that the work of an artist can be thought of in terms of a stylistic unfolding, where everything they paint before this image is inevitably a stylistic forerunner to what follows. But few artists, in fact, display this type of progression; the reality is always more messy and contradictory.

Finally, a clinical psychiatrist may approach Van Gogh's *Self-Portrait* as evidence that may help in understanding insanity. The psychiatrist may be interested in comparing this picture with other examples of Art by insane people, or with how Art may be used to alleviate the symptoms of insanity. This approach rests upon the assumption that the artist was insane (and this is far from being settled) or even that he was insane when this image was produced.

The point of detailing such approaches to the *Self-Portrait* is not to discredit them, but rather to show that our simple definition of History put forward at the beginning of this section is grossly inadequate. History is neither the regular and even accumulation of events through time, nor is it something that is fixed and therefore knowable simply by consulting 'the record'. What one gains from History is dependent upon what one puts into it. If one holds to a model of Art which sees it as essentially a vehicle for the expression of the artist's personality, then one will examine a work in those terms having taken into the past an already worked out model of artistic production. Such models and assumptions are the bases upon which all types of historical knowledge are constructed. Once again, I must stress that my aim is not to dismiss any particular approach to the History of Art, but rather it is the more general point that the best historians are those who *know* the premises they are operating with and carry into the past assumptions that have been subjected to careful scrutiny.

The conclusion that follows from this is that there can be no such thing as *the History of Art* with a set of absolute historical explanations, rather there are *Histories of Art* that are constructed using models which historians put together in their present and then transport into the past.

Story and narrative in History

Having established there are always Histories of Art, we have to ask the question, 'How are histories put together?' How do Art Historians make their histories?

At both the secondary and tertiary levels of education, most students acquaint themselves with accounts of Art History written by professional Art Historians. They familiarise themselves with what are referred to as *secondary sources*. It is the task of professional historians to confront the *primary sources* and to work such evidence into an account, either in the form of a book or an article in a scholarly journal. This sounds like a reasonably straightforward task until one actually encounters the primary sources.

My own experience can be called on here — one of my areas of interest is 19th-century photography and in the course of doing some research I visited a collection in the USA. The room in which the collection was housed had ten large cabinets with each cabinet holding ten to fifteen boxes. In all these was something between 30,000 to 50,000 photographs. The immediate feeling when confronted with so much 'evidence' is panic, followed by some serious decisions as to what to include as primary sources and what to exclude.

But the opposite can also be the case. A researcher may be able to locate only a handful of examples of the work of a particular artist or historical period and is faced with the task of constructing an account on very little evidence. In both situations a move is made from the evidence to the construction of an historical account or explanation. How is such a move possible and what is the nature of this entity 'an historical account' to which I have been referring to?

I want to answer these questions using the experience I've culled from teaching Art History. For a number of years I was responsible for delivering a set of introductory lectures on 20th century Art to first-year university students. I have not calculated the precise number of slides that were shown throughout the year; which is an infinitesimal amount compared to even the total output of a handful of the most respected artists of the 20th century. Teaching would never be effective if the lecturer were to approach the topic literally, that is by simply displaying slides of artists' works with no commentary. In order for teaching to commence examples have to be chosen and this selection then has to be incorporated into an account, that is a narrative/story. The result (hopefully) is an integrated and meaningful whole where images and words complement one another and make sense of the topic being studied. So in answer to my second question, 'What is an historical account?', I would reply simply that it is a narrative which attempts to explain, or make sense of, the past. As to the first question, 'How is the construction of an account possible, or what does it entail?', I would have to say that it is very similar to what takes place in all story-telling with a few crucial differences. At its simplest, a story consists of a beginning, a middle and an end. But if you cast your mind back to my confrontation with those 30,000 photographs from the 19th century it was exactly those features of story that were absent and which needed to be woven into the evidence in order to give it shape and structure and for it to make sense to us. Without that structure they remain, quite literally, un-accounted for. History then becomes an encounter between *evidence* and making sense of it through *narration*.

If we return to the situation of putting together a course on 20th-century art what happens is that particular art works are included and a vast number are excluded and the narration then becomes the way in which the included are placed into a set of meaningful relationships with one another. Words are not peripheral to this exercise, they are a medium through which relationships and interpretation are constructed. Once again we must recognise the existence of plurality, of there being a number of stories that can be made out of the enormous quantity of artistic material. What is important for the historian to be aware of is the principles upon which the inevitable process of inclusion/ exclusion is taking place; the fact that the Histories (the narratives) being told are being spoken from the present; lastly that the stories being told can never be final. So long as human beings are a species moving through time the making and the telling of History will never end.

Differential Histories

Students who have already had some kind of encounter with Art History, particularly with 20th-century art, will be familiar with the story that is told. A cursory glance at the titles of the books which survey the art of this period will reveal how strongly this idea of narrativity is present.
- *The Story of Modern Art*
- *The Rise of Abstract Art*
- *The Triumph of American Painting*
- *How New York Stole the Idea of Modern Art*

The 20th century — according to one's view on the matter — commences with the Impressionists in the late-19th century. Some Art Historians would even push the time of the Modern further back into the earlier part of the 19th century with the rise of Romanticism. However, having once established one's starting-point the story moves on to detail the 'breakthroughs' made by a handful of artists, as the principles of visual representation adhered to in European civilisation since the Renaissance are systematically overturned. The historical period is broken up into artistic movements — the 'isms' — which are seen as consisting of a set of unfolding stylistic shifts in painting and sculpture. These shifts are interpreted as evidence of a move further and further away from the Art of 'figurative representation'. It is a story in which major artists — Picasso, Braque, Malevich, Pollock — push back the boundaries of Art by producing works of extraordinary novelty.

Such an account is by now well known and exciting as it is (it's a good story), the new ways of thinking about History and Art History have cast doubts on its validity as an adequate account of what took place. But beyond this dispute about the truth value of 'the story', there is the feeling that this may only be one of many such possible accounts of which this is the most superficial in the sense of being an account of the surface of events only. Perhaps the most important idea to enter our thinking about History in the past few years is really a very simple one, namely that 'History' is not made up of a set of discrete events that continuously and regularly unfold within a common time frame. Rather historical time is not the same as clock-time, but is in fact made up of different sorts of movements through time. What we term History does not always happen *in* or *at* the same time, nor is History the equivalent of a column of men marching in step. Figure 2 should help to make this clearer.

If we imagine History as a series of different time scales roughly equivalent to radio wavelengths — then it is possible to take a *cut through* at a particular point on the time line. For any one such 'cut through' we will encounter different historical wavelengths, or we may decide to move horizontally through time but remain on a single wavelength. In terms of Art History we could say that the topmost layer consists of the most visible of events, individual artists making works of Art. But below this we may encounter longer lasting historical phenomena such as the consistencies of style, for example Neo-Classicism, or Romanticism. Below this we might encounter the collective cultural conventions about what a visual representation should consist of, that is the representation of physical objects in three-dimensional space. Even lower down we could look at such things as the shape of the image, the necessity for a flat surface for the image to rest on, the frame, and so on. At the most profound level of our section we may find those structures governing the very nature of symbol-making itself.

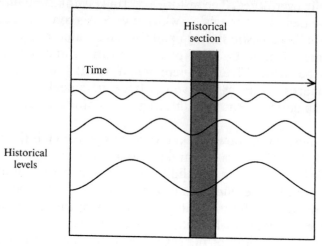

Figure 2

Whichever level historians choose to operate on is going to have great influence on how they see the past and particularly how they decide to divide it up into epochs or periods. (This process is called 'periodisation'.) If we return to our story of the 20th century, concentration upon the topmost level — the short wavelength — will tend to lead to the historian dividing the period off into clusters of events which are most visible, artists making novel stylistic breakthroughs. However, if one chooses to sink below this level it is quite likely that what at first appeared to be a radical change in the practice of Art was in fact resting upon profound continuities that have hardly shifted for centuries.

Once again we reach our familiar conclusion that History is not a unified and single entity. The possibility of there being different Histories to tell will depend upon which wavelengths one decides to trace out.

Conclusion

It would perhaps be helpful if I brought this chapter to an end by suggesting a few support systems for the student to use in this exercise.

From the outside it may often appear that the professional Art

Historians are engaged in debates equivalent in status to the medieval ones concerning the number of angels that could dance on the head of a pin. Single words such as 'expression', 'representation', or 'the real', often trigger argument and discussion of frightening intensity. Behind much of this lies the fact that the discipline of Art History is going through a process that is referred to as *a paradigm change*. What this means is that the normal channels of operation of the discipline start to break down and be replaced by a new set. Everything in the previously 'normal' state of the paradigm of Art History
• what its purposes and aims were thought to be
• what kinds of knowledge it could aspire to
• the rules whereby such knowledge could be attained
• the boundaries of its area of study
• even the nature of the area of study
all these essential components for 'normal Art History' begin to disappear. When an intellectual discipline enters this condition, the words or phrases it uses − let alone the ideas which stand behind them − begin to become areas of disputation and debate. What had previously been regarded as fixed, certain, or generally established, start to be questioned, so that all those easy habits of thought, speech and writing start to be revealed for what they very often were, just easy habits.

In the face of such change it becomes even more necessary that the student wishing to study the Fine Arts be able eventually, to make a set of informed choices about the intellectual approach they wish to use. In other words for as long as the paradigm change persists there will be a necessity for theory. Why is this?

In situations of paradigm change working in a particular discipline is no longer a 'natural' activity − albeit one that still requires years of training. That is, one just doesn't 'do' Art History, but becomes sensible to the fact that one has to construct *the tools* whereby one is then able to do Art History. Theory is simply the intellectual tools whereby one sets out to achieve a number a tasks (or fail!). Of course, the actual situation is more complex than this because − to continue the analogy − the tools may be faulty or the wrong ones, let alone the fact that one's attention is constantly being diverted by numerous travelling salesmen all claiming that they can equip you with a better and more efficient set.

So *theory* or thought is something which is an integral part of the activity one is engaged in and perhaps the most important assumption in this book is the belief that the more one knows what it is that one is doing, the better will be the end result.

The time has now arrived to begin to introduce the theory which informs the remainder of this book.

1

Why theory?

There is a traditional response on the part of students to the word 'theory' in any area, but it is particularly heartfelt in the case of the Visual Arts. The negative connotations clustering around the word 'theory' are not difficult to trace:

- theory is usually opposed to practice, with the former being seen as dry, intellectual and mental, whilst the latter is warm, rich, humane and fun
- theory is regarded as having a parasitical relationship to practice, which is the 'real thing', whilst theory is a crippling codification of something that is essentially anarchic, disparate and fluid
- practice is life, theory comes after life

Beneath each one of those contrasts where practice is played off against theory, lies a deeply entrenched cultural fiction which sets the 'heart' against the head, but always to the advantage of the heart. The difficulty with such emotional oppositions is that they are all too neat; it is as if our activities were divided into those that are all pure 'doing' against those which are all 'thinking'. One rather obvious, but often overlooked fact, is that everyone is a 'theoretician' in some form or another. By the time that you encounter a book such as this one you are already Art theoreticians, or more accurately, individuals who have 'thoughts' about Art, of a considerable degree of sophistication. The difficulty is that these thoughts are not referred to as 'theory', they are simply there, constituting an apparently natural part of the making or studying of the Fine Arts. The Italian thinker, Antonio Gramsci, captured the hidden nature of this theory when he wrote:

> It is essential to destroy the widespread prejudice that philosophy is a strange and difficult thing just because it is the specific intellectual activity of a particular category of specialists or professional and systematic philosophers. It must first be shown that all men are 'philosophers', by defining the limits and characteristics of the 'spontaneous philosophy' which is proper to everybody. This philosophy is contained in; 1. language itself, which is a totality of determined notions and concepts and not just of words grammatically devoid of content; 2. 'common sense' and 'good sense'; 3. popular religion and, therefore, also in the entire system of beliefs, superstitions, opinions, ways of seeing things and of acting, which are bundled together under the name 'folklore'.[1]

Gramsci is drawing our attention to the fact that as we grow up into a world inevitably we acquire a set of meanings and beliefs about a world. In the last chapter we saw how the word 'Art' is not simply a label which is attached to a set of recognisable objects, but is something of a much more active nature. It carves out, distinguishes and classifies these objects from other objects. As a word it exists in a system of connotations, associations and feelings of either a negative or positive nature. So language is always more than a set labels for things which already exist 'out there', rather it is a dynamic system through which we collectively construct a web of relationships that *is* our world.

In addition to acquiring language, without which we would be 'theory-less', we also acquire those elementary building blocks of experience without which the world would be inchoate and disparate. At this level, thought or theory, is made up of a whole continent of ideas, assumptions and givens about what our world consists of and how it functions. As Gramsci emphasises, this 'world' is all about us, in our stories (that is the devices we use in order to combine things and events together into meaningful entities), in our myths and our fears. Lastly it resides in our ideas about what it is to be human. Much of this material will always remain below the level of consciousness, or rather will appear overwhelmingly natural, an inevitable part of the landscape. It is something one thinks *with* but hardly ever thinks *about*.

Whatever the initial reaction to the word 'theory' might be — horror or delight — it is clear that by the time this reaction takes place that person is already committed to the use and making of theory. As you move through the remainder of the book there will be a constant switching from the 'spontaneous philosophy' mentioned by Gramsci to the more systematised activity of theory proper. What we have then is a three-stage operation that aims to:

* Highlight the thought that is already there
* Transform this pre-existing thought into a more organised and coherent form
* Enable the students to generate their own pathways across the area under consideration

This introductory text aims to help the reader move from being a passive and unwitting bearer of Art Theory into an active producer of it.

The model

The word 'model' seems the most fitting way of describing the type of theory I have in mind; that is something which approximates to a blueprint or a figure of operation. Such a model aims to aid explanation, not make evaluative judgements, so it will not demonstrate how 'good Art' or 'bad Art' is produced, but it might help in explaining why and how some Art comes to be regarded as good or bad.

This model, consisting of two types of components will provide the basis for the remainder of the book (Fig. 1.1).

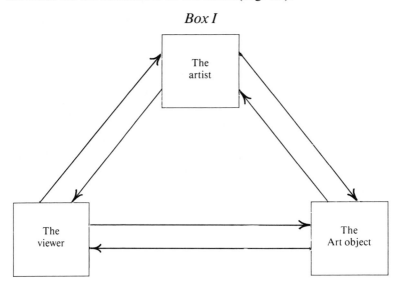

Figure 1.1

When viewed as a whole the figure is circular and I will call this *the aesthetic circuit*. As the book progresses each of the boxes will be examined in greater detail together with their reciprocal links.

The boxes

The boxes represent the concrete and observable elements which we would expect to be present under 'normal operating conditions'. So there are the makers, *artists*. There are the objects made, *works of Art*. And finally those who look at the works of Art, *the viewers or spectators*. It is important that we designate these three elements from the outset for the figure to be an accurate representation of the complete aesthetic circuit. However, it should be stressed that for any particular situation that we might want to examine it is quite possible for only a portion of the elements to be present. For instance, a spectator may encounter a work of Art produced by an unknown artist.

The boxes, whilst corresponding to actual, observable entities, are also meant to designate places within a structure. The boxes then are a way for us to sort out the rich complexities of actual situations into some preliminary kind of order. For example an individual may be an artist, a taxi-driver, a mother, and as a hobby collect stamps. The box is only concerned with those aspects of their lives which are brought into play when they engage in the activity of making Art. Likewise the spectator may exhibit a wide range of interests, but the third box is only concerned with those elements which are brought into play when they engage in the activity of looking at works of Art. The boxes therefore correspond to *positions* within an overall structure. The boxes should be thought as places for occupation rather than actual events. In order to engage in the activity of Art, be it making or looking, means taking up a particular position within this structure. Likewise the production of a work of Art means producing a particular sort of object which sits in the position assigned to it by the structure of the aesthetic circuit.

Each box begins by corresponding to actual entities but we need a depth model of each box in order to be able to represent the *complexity and multi-levelled nature* of each position. As we encounter each of the boxes what will happen will be a gradual working downwards from the surface level of commonsense to the deeper levels and processes that constitute each of these positions.

Box I — the artist
This will be concerned with only those processes that are engaged with during *the production of a work of Art*. The alternative label *artistic production* is more precise because we see that when artists make works of Art they participate in a particular set of organised processes which are both historically and socially determined.

Box II — the Art object
The Art work will be considered along two interconnecting axes. The first will split the Art work internally and look at the various dimensions which, when placed together, constitute the full complexity of this type of object. These levels are the work of Art as a *material object*, the work of Art as a *symbolic object*, and the work of Art as a *commodity*. This gives us a differentiated and complex object (Fig. 1.2).

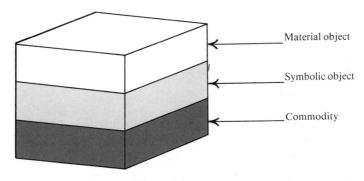

Material object

Symbolic object

Commodity

Figure 1.2

For Box II further distinctions still need to be made. An Art work may have a particular meaning or significance for the artist but when it leaves the studio it becomes a public object. Then it is seen by a variety of spectators who may interpret the work in ways very different from those which the artist intended for the work. Even the artist may come to view it differently after the Art work has had a career in the public domain. So we need to make the further distinction between *the object produced and the object seen*.

Box III — the spectator
Throughout the book this box will be referred to by many terms.

The reader will encounter the following titles — spectator, viewer, audience, reader, and subject and these terms will be more finely differentiated in the final section of the book. Here what is being referred to are the processes which any individual engages in when that person both sees a particular work of Art and attempts to make some sense of it. An apparently simple operation is again a complex and elusive process.

The double-headed arrows

While grasping the significance of each of the boxes, do not regard these as isolated and autonomous entities. The boxes represent the points within the aesthetic circuit where *reciprocal exchanges* are possible and the arrows indicate that such exchanges are operating.

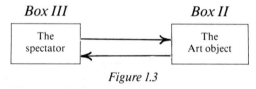

Figure 1.3

(*Note* — I have separated the arrows in this instance for clarity. Throughout the remainder of the book they will be designated by a double-head.)

Examine Figure 1.3. There is a long-standing debate in matters aesthetic as to the degree to which an Art object determines the interpretations which are made of it by the audience/spectator, against the claim that every encounter between the object and its spectator is a unique one, capable of generating completely fresh interpretations. Does the object precipitate the interpretation or does it originate with the spectator? In terms of the above figure this could be represented by either arrow and both should be retained until a decision is reached. According to how one sees this relationship between Art work and spectator, then one may wish to stress the autonomy of the work and so construct an interpretation of the work which sees it as able to rise above the particular conditions of time and place of its viewing and the particular social characteristics of the person who is doing the looking. The opposite theory, stressing the importance of time, place and the particularities of the viewer might wish to highlight the *differences* of interpretation. It will claim that only by taking into account such factors can we ever really begin to grasp what that work has meant to all the different types of audiences which have and will encounter it. Now it can be seen that the arrows involve the very nature of the boxes. Clearly in the example just given a specific view of the Art work (Box II) also involves a set of ideas about the content of Box III — the spectator.

At first it is best to think of the model as a static representation of an aesthetic circuit made up of a set of boxes linked by arrows but with the overall figure resting in a roughly contemporaneous time scale. Thus we might use the figure to plot the emergence of a particular Art work from its moment of production through to its audience's initial encounter with it — that is what interpretations are made of it when it first appears in the gallery. However, the model can only begin to deliver a plausible explanation if it is able to approximate in its structure to the situation 'out there' and that means that it must be able to register the passing of time. So as the figure is moved across time every element — the content of the boxes as well as the relationships between them — will be subject to change. For instance, the simple designation of a person as 'an artist' has undergone enormous shifts in meaning in the history of European Art and it was only towards the end of the 19th century that the term 'an artist' began to acquire anything like its contemporary meaning. It is precisely because of this variation that each of the boxes has to be unpacked in order to locate a more substantial core of attributes upon which we can rest our analysis. But it is also the case that the relationships between the boxes will fluctuate with the passage of time — it cannot assume that everything that *we* designate as Art has come into being through a set of similiar operations or that these have always belonged to the same class of objects.

If we examine each of the three Art works (ills 6, 7, 8) in terms of the relationship that holds between Box I and Box II, then it is clear that all three have come into being via very different routes. The Duchamp in illustration 6, apart from its irritating placement on the studio floor, has no physical relationship with the artist, purely a mental one in that it was chosen, but not made, by him. The religious icon in illustration 7, manifests a high level of manual skill imparted to it by a master craftsman, but is also the product of a highly conventionalised set of expectations as to what such an object should look like. It cannot be read as encapsulating a high degree of its maker's individuality. The final image, Schiele's *Self Portrait* (ill. 8) is characterised by a high degree of manual skill, whilst it carries a strong connotation of personal statement, of being something that speaks of a highly intense and intimate relationship between itself and the individual who made it. The lesson to be gleaned from this is that whenever the model is placed into a specific historical situation no presumptions can be

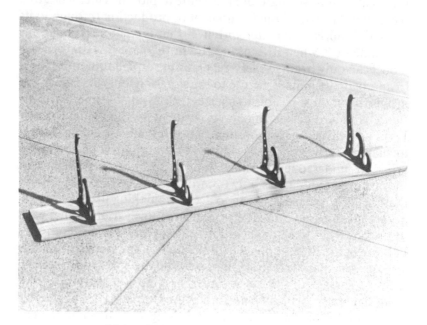

6. Marcel Duchamp: *Trébuchet (Trap)* 1917

made as to the *content* of the boxes and arrows, this, as always remains a matter of careful research. What I would claim however, is that whilst the content of the boxes and their relationships may alter, *the form* of the figure (its various components) will provide a consistent model of the aesthetic circuit operating at any time.

I will end this introduction to the diagram with one final example to show how it can be of help in enabling students to order

7. Byzantine mosaic: *Christ Eleemon* (Staatliche Museen, Berlin)

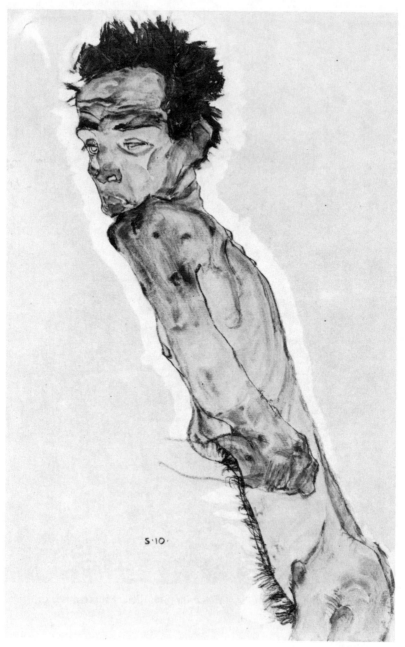

8. Egon Schiele *Self Portrait* 1917 (Lichtbildwerkstätte, Alpenland)

9. Giorgione/Titian: *Le Concert Champêtre c.*1508 (Louvre, Paris).
(The attribution of the work is disputed)

10. Antoine Watteau: *Fête champêtre c.*1750
(Staatliche Kunstsammlungen Dresden)

11. Edouard Manet: *Le déjeuner sur l'herbe* 1863 (Louvre, Paris)

12. Record cover for *Go Wild in the Country* 1981
(Courtesy BMG Records, UK)

their approaches to the study of the Visual Arts. This time I will focus upon Box II — the Art object.

Each of the paintings above (ills 9, 10, 11) utilises a theme which has had a long history in European Art. This is the *Fête Champêtre*, a form of idealised picnic. The work by Manet, *Déjeuner sur L'Herbe* (1863), is a variation upon this theme and consists of a re-working of the visual conventions which together constitute the theme, or the tradition, of the *Fête Champêtre*. It follows that the theme of this painting has a history independent of Manet, the artist. He intersects with this theme (or set of visual conventions) in 1863 and in order to produce the work of that year he re-activates this theme. He does not invent the theme but re-works this traditional theme in a new way. We could say that the conventions of the *Fête Champêtre* both enable him to produce this particular work, while constraining him to produce his image within a certain range of possibilities. Again we see the necessity for the presence of two arrows here in order to be able to represent the dual nature of the transactions between the artist and the themes contained within any particular visual tradition.

But the theme of the *Fête Champêtre* did not end there. It re-appeared on the record cover in illustration 12.

At first the model will be confining and undoubtedly you will feel as if it is constraining the free flow of your ideas. But as you become used to it, it should begin to allow you to quickly determine precisely where to place the type of questions you want to ask of artists, Art works, and their spectators.

1. Antonio Gramsci *Selections from the Prison Notebooks* London: Lawrence and Wishart, 1971, p. 323.

2
Producing Art and producing artists

Both the figure of the artist and the process of making Art have been a recurrent theme in Art itself as well as the site for communal mythologising. The cartoon in illustration 13 would seem to confirm the fact that there is already in circulation a complex set of ideas, as to what the makers and the making of Art are like. A remarkable degree of similarity can be found in such cartoons over the past 100 years in that they almost always represent Art and artists as being very different from other areas of life. The artist is nearly always depicted as being a peculiar kind of person, engaged in dubious kinds of work. Someone who makes objects incomprehensible to both their buyers and their public.

I want to use these stereotypes of Art and artists as a jumping-off point for this chapter and examine the ways in which Art *is different* from other areas of social life (the cartoon view) but also how it *is similar*. So far I've been using ideas and language which stress the similarities that Art and artists have with the rest of life and I have deliberately referred to Art as the *making* of a particular type of object — the Art object — and those engaged in this activity of making as artists.

Even to suggest that Art is a type of *work* is contrary to those stereotypes of Art and artists which surface in the cartoon. Words like 'work' or 'production' situate Art in the mundane world of the everyday, pointing to the similarities between it and other forms of making. It matters not whether representations of Art-as-different are positive in nature — Art as the result of exalted inspiration — or negative in the sense of the activity and the object evidencing no

" They've hung it upside down."

13. Daily Sketch June 1966
(with kind permission of Associated Newspapers Group)

sign of physical effort — on both counts Art is marked off as being different. If we keep this distinction between *maker* and *making*, or *producer* and *production*, then it becomes possible to internally differentiate Box I more closely (*see* Fig. 2.1).

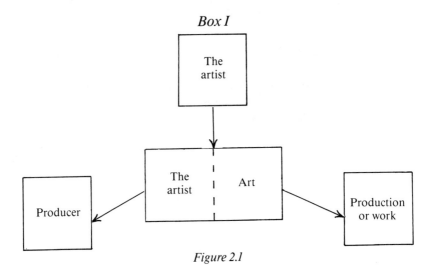

Figure 2.1

Adopting a more rational approach I think that my claim that Art involves work and is a type of production will be seen to contain some self-evident truths: the similarities first and then the differences.

Production and work in Art

When looked at from the perspective of work it is clear that some types of Art have involved the artist in extensive and taxing physical labour or at least have required *someone* to expend a lot of energy (*see* ill. 14). It is also clear that many types of Art, whilst not requiring large expenditures of physical labour, do demand very high levels of manual skills and dexterity, for example, sculpture, ceramics and tapestry weaving (*see* ill. 15). Other works can evince very little evidence of either physical labour or manual skill on the part of the artist (*see* ill. 16). To understand the bewildering varieties of Art objects and the great range of methods used to

14. Christo: *Little Bay, Sydney* 1970

15. Sydney sculptor Simeon Nelson, 1989
(Photograph permission of the artist)

make them we need a complex model of production. All *produc-tion* consists of physical work and mental work. Art production is special, though not unique, in always having a strong mental

16. Carl André: *Sixteen Pieces of Slate* 1967

component allied to a variety of manual and physical skills. It is the way in which they are *combined together* within the making process that in the past has been responsible for the differences between 'normal work' and 'artistic work', although this is a matter of degree, not of absolute difference.

If we examine the concept of simple work more closely it can be seen to consist of three elements which are united in one process.

A	*B*	*C*
Physical matter ⟶	Physical and mental labour ⟶	The object

Figure 2.2

The whole sequence adds up to the *work process.*

The class of objects which are produced by the *work process of Art* differ from the objects of normal making in that the artist is producing things whose symbolic content normally outweighs their utilitarian function. I would hold to this assertion but it does require a certain degree of qualification — there are a class of makers who are not normally classified as artists but who produce symbolic objects, for example, signwriters. Other makers may have their activity classified as 'craft'. Here the objects produced can have a utilitarian function and at the same time also carry a symbolic significance. Finally there is the historical problem in that individuals who are *today* classified as artists were in their own time, responsible for making a wide range of 'non-Art' objects. For instance, the German painter Lucas Cranach the Elder (1472-1553) was typical for his time. Not only did he paint pictures, he was also responsible for designing the court clothes of his employer, organising public festivals, as well as designing the shields for the court militia. Despite such qualifications, I think we can define the process of artistic production as the transformation of physical matter, through the work performed by the artist, into symbolic objects.

Artistic production as a social activity

No social collectivity or culture can exist for very long without its members expending energy, in the form of work, in either physical and/or mental forms. Such expenditures of energy are always organised into collective or social patterns. Random and spontaneous outbursts of work on their own would quickly lead to a collapse of social life, so there have always been ways in which individual expenditures of energy are integrated into a set of *organised and collective work processes*. For instance, work will be undertaken in particular places and for defined lengths of time. So work as a transformatory operation (making) will be rule governed. It is not a spontaneous or arbitary set of activities. Yet in many ways it is precisely such terms as 'spontaneous', 'arbitary' and 'individual' which seem to encapsulate the stereotypes which are in circulation about how Modern Art is produced. Like all myths this view only captures part of the truth. One need only think of activities such as ceramics — where high degrees of manual skill are essential, or film making where production rests upon a collective effort requiring complex systems of organisation, to see how partial such myths as this are. As always in the analysis of Art, a knowledge of its history will show that the processes of making symbolic objects has varied immensely. We can illustrate this by focusing on the *forms* taken by artistic production. It is clear that all societies have undertaken work in a general sense, and also that such societies seem to have produced objects with a symbolic significance, but the ways in which these objects have been produced has varied enormously.

The *Abelam* are a people living in the Sepik River area of New

Guinea. In their traditional way of life one of the centrepieces of their symbolic production was the building of large, highly decorated ceremonial houses by the men of the clan. The task of building a new ceremonial house was an activity in which all of the men participated, working together. There was a degree of 'artistic specialisation' as certain individuals who were known to be especially skilled in carving and painting were assigned particular tasks. The shape of the building, the details of its construction and the symbols deployed in the paintings were *known* by all the members of the clan and the artists' had to work within certain limits. Each stage of the house's construction was accompanied by ceremonial and ritual observances which were considered an essential component of the building process itself. When the work was completed the builders returned to their everyday tasks. Symbolic production was an activity which was collective, public and involved only intermittent bouts of specialised activity.

In medieval Europe we find that artistic production was organised differently. All 'Art' making was conducted within guilds, hierarchical associations which specialised in the production of certain objects. These were, in fact institutions whereby manual skills were both protected and transmitted on to a new generation.

Guilds resembled extended families and young apprentices were 'adopted' into the house of the master craftsmen and treated like junior family members. In order to qualify as professional artists, apprentices had to complete a course of instruction which was laid down in detail in the guild's regulations. An apprenticeship would take several years during which time the various aspects of the craft would be imparted to the novice in the workshops of the particular guild.

Production within these guild structures was different from that which we imagine as the normal route for Art to appear. It was not unusual for many people to have a hand in the production of single oil painting. One apprentice might have been assigned the task of preparing the colours or priming the canvas. Assistants might have taken responsibility for particular elements of the picture, for instance one may be good at clouds, another drapery. The master might have been responsible for the overall composition together with certain elements within the image. The final work was the outcome of a bewildering (for us) number of contributions.

Arnold Hauser in his book *The Social History of Art* sums up the general features of guild production in the following way:

> The artist's studio of the early Rennaissance is still dominated by the communal spirit of the mason's lodge and the guild workshop: the work of art is not yet the expression of an independent personality, emphasising his individuality . . . Until the end of the 15th century the artistic labour process still takes place entirely in collective forms.[1]

So the guild system of artistic production was *a collective form* organised around a *permanent specialisation* of a particular set of manual skills. Both of these modes of artistic production, the traditional Abelam system, and that of the Guilds, are very different to those of Contemporary Art where seemingly *autonomous individuals* make symbolic objects in accordance with a set of rules which are apparently of a personal nature and where artistic production is regarded as a life-long vocation. The above examples show that in certain societies the processes for making symbolic objects can be similar to other adjacent areas of production. (In the case of traditional tribal societies the *difference* is not a difference of technology or the actual work processes, rather that the task has a magico-religious significance.) However, when we look at societies which started to become dominated by industrialised methods of production, as Europe was in the 19th century, the making of Art objects starts to be organised and understood in different ways to that of general production. Here, Art production, was begun to be seen as an activity with a high degree of individual control of the making process and with this increase in individual responsibility came ideas about the maker as somehow being a different type of person from those whose manual skills had been absorbed into factory production. Very often the sorts of skills retained by artists were archaic, or derived from pre-mechanised modes of production (oil painting and sculpture). The net result of this shift was to make it appear that artists were not really involved in a process of 'work' at all.

These disturbances in the relationship between artistic production and general production have entailed periodic feelings of dissatisfaction within artists themselves. Some have responded to these changes by attempting to revert to earlier modes and techniques of Art production by espousing programs of productive fundamentalism. For instance, the 19th-century artist William Morris (1834-1896) became highly critical of modern, de-humanised systems of production. His ideal was the working methods of the medieval guilds which were seen as potentially more humane and more democratic because they allowed for a true integration of individual expression and artistic materials. To this end he set up workshops where he hoped to revive the spirit of guild production. Closer to the present day, the Italian artist Giorgio di Chirico (1888-1978) underwent a profound disillusionment with Modern Art and its supporting technologies. Not only did the style of his paintings swing back to those of the Italian Renaissance, he also began to re-utilise the techniques by which the old masters had prepared their paints in the hope of circumventing what he saw as the corrupting influences of Modernism.

Almost always the leap back to earlier modes of production is coupled to ideas that the modern ways of making Art are debilitating, alienated or ineffectual. Regression is seen as a way to regenerate Art, to provide it with a firmer social purpose or simply as a way of enabling the artist to achieve a higher degree of personal authenticity in their work.

A move can be made in the other direction with artists adopting the most modern technological methods of working as a sign of their desire to leave behind the archaic trappings of Art production. For instance, the sculptors of the immediate post-revolutionary period in the USSR incorporated new materials into their work as well as attempting to scientifically define the rules for the production of the new work. Ironically, many of the reasons given for the backward journey are the same as those who enthusiastically espouse the new.

Producing artists

Return to Figure 2.1 on page 45 and look at the other half of our initial division in Box 1 − *the artist*. It is true that there have always been instances of individuals who might be called 'born artists', or 'naive artists', but it is also the case that there have always been social mechanisms for producing artists. (Even Picasso, the great 'natural' of Modern Art, was the son of an artist and attended art school in Barcelona.) In traditional tribal societies individuals who display particular manual skills or certain personality traits, or who just happen to inherit the role, are recruited to take on the tasks of making symbolic objects. The guild system of production was a complex mode for recruiting and training individuals into the particular set of skills lodged in the guild. The modern system for producing artists only begins to be put into place in Western Europe towards the end of the 19th century. The responsibility for the training of artists starts to be taken over by the State and local government which established special institutions for the production of artists — the art schools. Alongside of the creation of such Art training institutions were rules, both overt and covert, as to how individuals were to be recruited into the profession and how they were to be trained. These diffuse rules of recruitment fixed the range of people who were considered eligible to become artists and for a long time chief among such factors were *levels of educational attainment* and *gender.*

Since the setting up of State Art schools in the late 19th century, the level of education required of potential Art students has steadily risen. It is undoubtedly the case that artists in the 20th century are more highly educated that at any time in the past. This is commensurate with the increasing amount of mental labour contained within Contemporary Art. In order to gain access to Art training establishments a very high standard of education is demanded before entry is permitted — in most cases this is now seen as being the equivalent to entry into university. It also follows that an individual wishing to train in the Visual Arts must be able to acquire such preliminary educational standards before being allowed to embark upon an Art career. Many individuals from disadvantaged social groups will be unable to attain such standards in the same way that they are excluded from other educational openings. What is termed High Art has steadily became the province of the highly educated elites within modern societies — both in terms of its makers and its audiences.

It should also be clear from the illustrations and examples that I've used in the book so far — and despite a deliberate attempt, wherever possible, to furnish approximately equal examples — that the male of the species dominates the Visual Arts of the 20th century, as well as those of past times. It is here that we encounter social factors that operate after the point of initial recruitment. Compared with other professions such as law, science, or engineering, women have always been well represented in the recruits taken into the Art schools. Even in the 19th century a high percentage of women students (*see* ill. 17) was not unusual, nor is it so today. Despite this high percentage of women students, it remains the case that they have found it very much more difficult to translate this training into full-time professional careers.

17. Students of the National Gallery Art School, Melbourne, 1896 or 1897
(State Library of Victoria)

To understand this discrepancy between high rates of training
but relatively low full-time careers — even though the situation is
gradually changing — requires an explanation other than that of
biology. This gap appears to be caused by a combination of those
covert and overt rules within the general organisation of social life
that we mentioned earlier. It is still only with great difficulty that
women are able to successfully combine full-time careers with
marriage and raising a family. A career in Art demands a high
degree of social mobility and personal freedom but lacks many of
the supporting structures that may be available to women in other
professions. The making of Art is not well paid, particularly in its
initial phases and rests upon assumptions of autonomy and
rugged individualism. This is fine for men but very rough for
women who are still primarily responsible for child-rearing. Within the training institutions of Art processes of differential direct-
ing may be in operation. Certain mediums may be seen as being
'more appropriate' to women. Such switching mechanisms may induce feelings of profound frustration in many women who opt for
the 'safer' waters of Arts administration. Thus the categories of
lone male doers and females who organise the doers is reproduced

and perpetuated. Last, but not least, there is the continuing — some would say congenital — inability of men to regard the Art produced by women as being significant. The trivialisation of women's Art, its relegation as being 'minor', or 'not ambitious' can tax an individual to the point of refusing to participate at all.

In this chapter I have argued that much can be gained from looking at Art from the angle of work and production. It allows us to see it as a particular way of making a particular set of objects which have a symbolic meaning. I have also argued that the modern ways of organising Art production differ from the more general ways of making things in that it places a great deal of the responsibility about *what* should be made and *how* it should be made upon the individual. The artist becomes a specialist in the domain of the symbolic. This modern situation of Art and the artist was best summed by an English writer of the 19th century, William Hazlitt, who said that Art is 'a gregarious activity practised in private'.

Against this emphasis upon the individual maker, with all its advantages and anxieties, I have shown that the system for producing artists entails a network of institutions whose purpose is to recruit a set of trainees according to particular rules. Such collective modes of recruitment, despite their overt proclamations, are neither just nor fully democratic. Although in the process of change — hopefully ever more advanced when you read this book — the ways in which individuals gain access to careers in the Visual Arts and their successes and failures subsequent to leaving art school, still means that the making of Art remains a socially restricted and male-dominated activity.

1. Arnold Hauser *The Social History of Art* vol. II, London: Routledge and Kegan Paul, 1951, p. 48.

3
What is produced?

In the last chapter we looked at Art as a system of production, or organised work, which specialises in the making of symbolic objects together with the modern system for producing Art producers. Having looked at Art from the perspective of production it is now time to examine the nature of the thing which is made. In terms of the model we are now making the first move from Box I to Box II.

As with Box I, the initial entry into the second box begins at the level of commonsense, namely the existence of a 'thing' which is usually referred to as *the Art work* or *Art object*. However, just as in the case of the terms 'Art' and 'artist', the terms 'Art object' or 'Art work' point to a complexity existing beneath such straightforward designations. 'Art object' indicates the presence of a physical entity, something that can been seen and touched whilst 'Art work' refers back to the domain of production, something that has been worked on and refers forward in the sense of something that itself will work or function.

It is important to retain this idea of the Art object as a *complex entity*, because it is precisely this ensemble of characteristics which both establishes its similarity with other things-in-the-world and yet also marks it off as being different. In our earlier discussion of Art as production reference was made to the fact that what was particular to the Art object was its *symbolic nature*, this means that we can now identify at least two levels within the Art object — it is both a material object and a symbolic object. One remaining dimension needs to be added to this for us to be able to grasp the full complexity of the Art object. Many works of Art are able to command very high prices. Whilst these spectacular Art auctions are events which get the coverage of the media, it should be remembered that artists are human beings. They have material needs and occasionally like to have a drink, go to the cinema, and read newspapers. In order to satisfy these needs they prefer to sell their work rather than give it away. To do this they put a price, or economic value, on their Art works, hoping through such sales to be able to continue to paint, sculpt or make films. All this is rather obvious but I have mentioned it because often in the analysis of Art the emphasis focuses in upon the symbolic aspect, with the economic dimension being treated as if it were a rather shameful secret, best kept for discussion by those 'in the know'. The final dimension of the Art object that needs to be registered is that of the Art work as commodity — that is an object which can be bought or sold.

Our model of the Art work now looks like this:

Box II

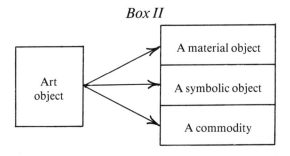

Figure 3.1

So the process of making a work of Art is an activity which produces a complex object. That is an object which consists of a *material* dimension, a *symbolic* dimension, and an *economic* dimension. We will attempt to answer the initial question 'What is produced?' by looking at each of these dimensions in turn, commencing with the material level of the Art object.

The work of Art as material object

We can best begin this section by recalling the three elements of the artistic process of production laid out in Figure 2.2, page 48 and

18. Henry Moore in the marble quarries at Querceta
(reproduced by kind permission of the Henry Moore Foundation)

19. Henry Moore: Artist at work
(reproduced by kind permission of the Henry Moore Foundation)

20. Henry Moore: *Reclining Figure* UNESCO, 1957-58
(reproduced by kind permission of the Henry Moore Foundation)

which can be seen in this simple sequence in operation in the work of an artist like Henry Moore (*see* ills. 18, 19, 20). However, in the vast majority of Art works such a direct and immediate transformation of physical matter is not so evident. For example in the production of stained-glass windows the artist is reliant upon additional processes for the production of glass, pigments and the metals which are brought together in the completed work. Even a technologically simple act like drawing depends upon industries to produce pencils and paper. In such cases there are *intermediate processes and technologies* which are drawn upon by the artist and then transformed by them into Art objects. In some instances it is other finished objects or images which provide the starting-point for the re-workings of the artist. For instance, Max Ernst utilised illustrations taken from late 19th-century scientific magazines which he subsequently re-worked in his collages, for example, *The Hat Makes the Man*.

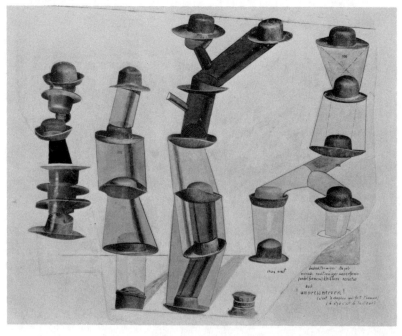

21. Max Ernst: *The Hat Makes the Man* 1920. Collage, pencil, ink and watercolour, 35.6 x 45.7 cm
(Collection, The Museum of Modern Art, New York)

The technologies of Art

All societies have existed in a physical environment made up of plants, animals, and the land. This physical environment presents itself to a society as a collection of possible resources which are also potential materials for the making of Art. No society has utilised every such potential source but has always made a precise selection from the total range of available materials. These 'selections' were rarely done on an individual basis, but were determined by the collective rules of the society which stressed the production of certain types of objects using certain sorts of materials. So distinctive were these cultural selections that archaeologists and anthropologists are often able to identify a particular society simply by the nature of the tool kit and equipment which it carried around with it. Cultural selection becomes equivalent to the thumbprint or signature of that particular way of life. One of the best ways to see this in operation is the range of pigments which are deployed within any one culture. In societies with simple technologies there may be only a few such pigments, resulting in the use of a strictly limited range of colours — black, white, and red are perhaps the most commonly recurring of these. Not only do the selection of pigments vary, but the range of materials utilised varies too. The greater the complexity of a culture's technology the greater the range of colours there are to draw upon. This reaches its apotheosis in industrial societies where Art production is able to avail itself of materials occuring on a global basis.

Few cultures have simply made Art directly from naturally occurring materials and even societies with simple technologies have elaborate techniques for transforming such materials into forms appropriate to the production of symbolic objects. The preparation of pigments involves a wide variety of techniques for the Abelam people of New Guinea,

> red, yellow, black and white . . . are the four traditional colours and the only colours recognised for ritual purposes; in some areas where European colours have been used they are subsumed into the traditional system, blue counting as black and green as yellow for instance. Yellow and white occur naturally, the first as small nodules of yellow ochre in the clayey soil in certain well-known sites; the nodules are broken up, washed and strained and the resulting fine powder dried and stored. The white occurs either in the form of a chalk-like stone in the beds of streams or as patches of earth in boggy ground, and is likewise powdered, washed and

stored. Red ochre is produced by heating a lignite-like substance that is found in certain parts of the Abelam area. It is placed on a pottery crock with some vegetable matter, including red flowers, and heated over a strong fire for some hours; the residue is washed and filtered and stored in the form of a fine powder. Black paint is neither stored nor traded, but made as required. Scrapings from the bottom of cooking vessels are chewed with sap from a tree related to breadfruit and some edible leaves, the resulting material is spat out into containers and has to be used at once since once it dries out it cannot be re-used.[1]

As the material equipment of a society increases, intermediate materials and technologies become employed and deployed in the production of Art. Pigments, papers, brushes, glass, metals, through to the highly sophisticated electronic and chemical technologies of the present day. Such changes in the nature of the intermediate materials available to artists can often produce quite dramatic alterations in such apparently slow changing forms like painting and sculpture.

Before the onset of paper-making in Europe (sometime during the 13th century) vellum or parchment was used to provide suitable surfaces upon which to write and paint, as seen in illuminated manuscripts. Vellum was made from the skins of calves or newly born lambs with only the softest part of the skin being selected. The raw skin was then subjected to a complex preparation process in which it was shaved, stretched, and dried. After being purchased for use in manuscripts it underwent even further preparation and the final result was a surface that was relatively impervious to ink and which 'took' the contemporary pigments used in illustrations. Vellum continued to be used even after the invention of paper in Europe because the early forms of medieval paper were friable and provided an inferior surface on which to write and draw. It was the introduction of the printing press which was to seal the fate of vellum as the most common material for book production. As the quality of paper improved, parchment use was restricted to luxury items only, eventually being confined to the preparation of legal documents.

Not only are the intermediate techologies of Art continually changing, they also interact with one another and an examination of the sequence in which they appear within any one culture is just as important in understanding the material base of Art as is the range of technologies that are available at any particular moment.

In 1856 Sir William Henry Perkin discovered how to produce

synthetic pigments from coal tar. These pigments, known as aniline colours were quickly taken up by the developing chemical industries of Europe — especially in Germany — and were made available in a form usable by artists. Although highly unstable in their initial forms — they tended to change colour when exposed to light and decayed over time — they were quickly adopted by the artists of the 19th century because of the enormous number of new colours that could be produced by this method and the intensity of the hues. The results on painting were to produce images that appeared 'too real' and 'too intense' to the viewers of the day. Another side-effect of this increasing industrialisation of the materials of Art was to end the necessity of the artist to learn the laborious, small-scale methods of manufacturing their pigments. By the end of the 19th century tuition in the preparation of materials was almost totally ignored in the training of Art students and artists became dependent upon the labour and skill of auxiliary specialists.

But if the rise of synthetic materials had the effect of displacing the old ways, it also opened up fresh opportunities. This was particularly intense in the practice of sculpture where, until the beginning of the 20th century, only a few materials were considered appropriate to the medium — stone, wood, plaster and bronze. It was in the movements of Futurism, Cubism and Constructivism that sculptors began to make use of the materials emanating from industrial processes — wire, steel, glass, aluminium, and later plastics all began to make an appearance in sculpture.

The introduction of new intermediate technologies and materials can clearly change 'the look' of a particular Art form, but they can also interact with other Art mediums whose technologies have remained relatively constant. For instance, there is the well-known 'interaction' between photography and painting where it can be seen that with the coming of the camera certain forms of painting — particularly those primarily used to record people, places and things — were rapidly rendered redundant by the properties of the photographic image and the technologies of photography. With the arrival of an ever-increasing range of synthetic materials and more sophisticated methods of electronic image reproduction and transmission such medium interactions have been more frequent than has been realised. The impact of plastics upon the craft and industry of ceramics would appear to parallel that of photography and painting, whilst the rise of the technologies of film and video has profoundly affected the way fiction is written. The *form* of the story would seem to have been irrevocably altered by the superior descriptive powers of these visual mediums.

Concern with the materiality of the Art object is still important, but today it is in the areas of historical and economic validation that such expertises tends to be deployed. For instance, the current vogue for historical reconstructions requires a detailed knowledge of the precise materials used as well as the techniques which were employed in their original production. Historical attribution, that is the determination of the time, the place and the individual artist, who made a particular work, has been greatly advanced by the devising of scientific techniques capable of an extraordinary detailed scrutiny of the physical composition of the Art object. The knowledge produced by such techniques of x-ray, chemical and spectrographic analyses is crucial to the conservation and restoration of the objects. These techniques for determining the physical composition of a work also bear directly upon the status of the Art object as a commodity in that it becomes easier to detect forgeries and fakes. Authenticity in the form of an accurate and trustworthy historical attribution is a crucial factor in the life of an Art work as an economic value

The one most important point to take away from this rudimentary survey of the material dimensions of the Art object is that all Art making rests upon a set of *material substrates*, each of which have their own distinctive histories. If you recall the model of differential historical wavelengths (Fig. 2, p. 28), these histories of Art's material substrates would lie at the very deepest levels. That these dimensions are so often overlooked or ignored in Contemporary Art Histories is due, I think, to the fact that the most frequent way in which we encounter Art objects today is in the form of reproductions. This tends both to evaporate the distinct material properties of the things and render them into a set of equivalences via the dominant visual technology, the photographic image. This rendering down of objects to the common coinage of the photograph makes it easier for us Moderns to treat the material and symbolic dimensions of an Art work as absolutely separate. This was not always so and in the past the particular stuff out of which the symbolic object was made tended to migrate across the material/symbolic dividing line and have important repercussions for what the object meant. The use of gold leaf in religious icons added to the spiritual preciousness of such images, while the utilisation of the finest woods, the best yarns and the most precious jewels all contributed to the symbolic value surrounding the work.

1. Anthony Forge 'Paint — a Magical Substance' *Palette* no. 9, Spring 1962.

4

The work of Art as a symbolic object

Recall the various levels of the Art object that we isolated in Figure 3.1 on page 57.

A material object
A symbolic object
A commodity

After the brief examination of the material dimension of the Art work undertaken in the last chapter we now need to move down to the second level and examine factors involved in the Art work as *a symbolic object*.

Signs, symbols, codes and conventions

A major difficulty in discussing this dimension of the work of Art is the plethora of terms which attempt to condense and describe what is involved in the symbolic function of the art object. The sectional title above indicates there are already four such related terms, each impinging upon this dimension of the art object.

The re-location of Art within a theory of signs, or semiotics is an important advance of the 1970s and 1980s. By effecting such a re-location, the Visual Arts have begun to be seen in relation to the more general findings about how signs function. Re-location has also positioned Art much more closely to sign systems that were previously seen as being radically different from those used in Art. The effect of these two shifts has been complex but one might say that initially the old *distinctiveness* of Art underwent dissolution, but new sorts of distinctiveness had begun to be formulated but always within a theory of signs in general. In order to detail this rather abstract assertion I will touch on a limited amount of its history clarifying various terms about the sign-nature of the work of Art.

Semiotics in essence is an attempt to describe and explain that feature of human social life which rests upon our ability to communicate with one another through the use of signs. This general level of communication implies that human beings are able to lead an inter-subjective existence by being able to transmit information via the various languages available in a given culture. For us to communicate we do not simply engage in thought transference but have to avail ourselves of *codes*. It is the existence of codes and their material manifestation in signs, which enables the process of information transmission to take place. Thus codes are, by their very nature, shared processes. The term 'code' always implies the existence of two individuals, a coder and a decoder. The re-location of the Visual Arts within a theory of signs has led to a view that sees the Art object as primarily a coded object. So for the term *symbolic object* substitute the term *coded object*.

If this were all that such a re-location entailed the remainder of this chapter might be straightforward. However, the analysis of signs is complex and must be considered at a general level before moving onto the particularities of the Visual Arts. One of the most widespread usages in the analysis of signs in the late 1980s is that formulated by the USA philosopher C. S. Peirce (1839-1914).[1] He begins with this definition of a sign

> it is something which stands to somebody for something in some respect or capacity[2]

There are at least four elements in his definition which are important for us:
- there is the sign which is 'standing in for'
- there is the something which is being 'stood-in-for'
- there is the somebody for whom the 'standing-in-for has relevance'
- there is the 'sense, or meaning', which the 'standing-in-for has for that person'

This definition comes close to the meaning that the word 'symbol' has in common usage and that element of 'standing-in-for-ness' is what we most readily associate with the word. Peirce goes beyond this general assertion about signs to specify different types of standing-in and this is the basis of his famous tripartite typology of signs in general. Signs may be subdivided into:

The icon — here the relationship between the sign and what it is standing-in-for is one of resemblance where the reader of the sign acknowledges that the sign has elements which *resemble* the thing it is standing in for. This should *not* be interpreted as a sign system based upon the existence of 'natural resemblances' between the icon and the object it stands in for. It is quite possible for an icon to stand in for an object which does not exist as the numerous paintings of angels in the Western tradition will testify. It is the act of interpretation by the viewer of the sign who reads the physical properties of the sign as if they were in an iconic relationship to the thing it stands in for.

The index — here there is an actual, concrete relationship between the sign and what it signals, for instance a knock at the door, or animal tracks.

The symbol — here the relationship between the sign and the object it stands in for is a matter of *convention* (in the technical parlance the relationship is *arbitrary*). Here the relationship between the sign and what it is standing-in-for is known by the viewer of the sign because they are in possession of the code, or the system of rules, which governs what will stand for what.

Peirce's typology of signs is applicable to many kinds of visual imagery. To generalise it might be said that the figurative pictures in the tradition of the West are iconic signs in that they have elements of resemblance with the objects they are standing in for. So strong is this tradition of reading visual signs that we talk constantly about visual images as if what was depicted were actually in front of us. Within visual images themselves we most frequently encounter a combination of icons and symbols, but 'indexicality', is also present in that frequently we interpret images as if the specific marks on canvas and paper were signs of the artist's personality. That signature in the corner often becomes the equivalent of a track left by the singular person who produced the image. For the remainder of the book I want the symbolic aspect of visual imagery to refer to the differential capacity of the marks, colours, shapes, forms, and other features placed on a two-dimensional surface to 'stand in for' another set of objects, ideas, emotions, and values. When we talk about the symbolic dimension of Art objects we are referring to that overall ability they have to stand in for, represent, evoke or depict other things.

Codes and coding

Although Peirce's typology establishes some very important features of the operations of signs in general, it needs supplementing. His definition of the sign interpreter was a singular individual, apparently unconnected to any other person. In certain circumstances a purely individual symbolism (or system of signs) may be in operation but we normally encounter sign systems which *circulate amongst a collection of people*. That is sign systems are shared and therefore in some way are communal. We need terms which capture this collective aspect of signs and here 'code' and 'coding' would seem appropriate.

Coding — the verb — refers to the activity engaged in to produce a set of meaningful signs. *Code* refers to the system of rules in circulation amongst a group, the use of which enables meaning to be possible. The word code also implies the ability to *decode* the meaningful signs which coding produces. So the terms *code* and *coding* always rely upon the assumption that there is a definable set of procedures which have to be engaged with in order to produce meaningful signs within a specific group.

Conventions

Much of the discussion so far is applicable to visual imagery but was initially formulated as a way of explaining the operations of language. The *distinctiveness* of the Visual Arts from other sign systems must be examined because there are still other dimensions in this area which are not easily explained by the very general terms we have utilised up to now. There is another term which will aid this move to visual sign systems — *Convention*.

Two factors would appear to justify this terminological addition. The first lies in the nature of visual imagery in general, the second with the nature of 'artistic' visual imagery.

Peirce's definition rests upon an idea of signs as individual units — one sign standing in for one object. This causes innumerable difficulties for visual imagery where it is difficult to isolate individual units/signs from the general field of the complete image. Visual imagery is, by definition, something we encounter instantaneously, not unit by unit and so it is the total field of an image's signs and *their relations to one another* that is their distinctive feature. What is needed is a way of talking about such broad features while retaining the advances in our understanding that sign and code have enabled. For instance, in Western and other traditions the use of a flat regular surface upon which marks are placed is a feature common to visual imagery, something we take for granted. Likewise the predominance within the post-Renaissance tradition, of the image adopting an iconic relationship to the scene it is depicting is commonplace. In both of these examples the general status and organisation of the image is a matter of *convention*, a generally accepted way of doing things. Likewise when we consider the practice of Art we immediately encounter, not a natural activity, but an activity which is highly rule-governed or conventional, such that both the producers, the viewers and the objects, interact and gain a meaning only if the rules and conventions are known and shared. This means that the conventions of Art are meaningful acts and objects within a set of particular cultural and historical circumstances, but they become meaningful only because they are coded.

The idea of coding and convention detailed above has enabled enormous advances to be made in the ways in which we conceptualise the making of Art and the status of Art objects. I would go further and say that this re-location of Art within a broader semiotic model has led to the redundancy of numerous ideas which deliberately obfuscated the process of artistic production in a set of vague and quasi-mystical formulations. The idea of coding is a direct reply to those who would turn Art making into an ineffable mystery in three ways. Firstly coding is largely, but not wholly, an unconscious process; secondly coding is a rule-governed activity; finally conscious choice can and does operate at certain levels of coding, but this in no way lessens the coded nature of what is being done. The implications which flow out of these assertions are that the processes of coding need not be fully known by each individual producer for them to be operative. The codes being engaged circulate amongst individuals of particular language communities which are in possession of the codes. Finally that coding operating at very deep levels does not exclude the role of individual choice at other levels. In fact one of the distinctive features of contemporary artistic production is the desire to push the consciousness of the artist deeper and deeper into the various levels of coding. Thus an Art work may situate itself at the very horizons of consciousness, that point where meaning is flickering on and off. On the other hand other works may sit happily with a high level of conscious coding with the artist playing a game of variations on a theme. At this point conscious decisions may be made about both the form and content of a statement — linguistic or visual — but it is not necessary for the rules through which such meaningful statements can emerge to be consciously recalled every time a code is utilised or a convention adhered to.

Summary

When artists make Art works they call up every other act of Art making that has preceded that instance of production. Not only is this history re-activated in the use of particular materials, but also in the manner in which the materials are deployed. These bodies of sedimented and codified knowledge concern themselves with what are the appropriate methods of undertaking the task in hand. This deposited knowledge is manifest in the physical effort (the particular skills) utilised as well as in the mental assumptions (conventions) and codes which constitute what an image is and how it can be meaningful or significant. For instance, handing on a manual skill from teacher to pupil is the reproduction in the eye, hand and musculature of the student of everything which that culture has managed to store to that point, and we often refer to this as *tradition*. Along with the physical and manual inheritance, the student is also ushered into a body of codes and conventions which ensure that the object made fulfils that culture's assumptions about what an Art work should be (or it may try to violate, or break with these assumptions). Conventionality, in this sense, denotes that dimension of the Art object which relies upon adherence to a body of cultural assumptions in order to be seen as belonging to the category of objects it aspires to join. At the deepest levels of the Art object one eventually reaches a point where the cultural and the natural intersect and intermingle. At these levels assertions concerning where one places a particular characteristic — in the realm of culture or in the natural — are harder and harder to make with any certainty. There is a point where tradition and conventionality seem to take on the force of a 'second nature'. The wish to make visual symbols of whatever kind, for instance, would appear to be a universal human characteristic.

Now we must move towards a closer examination of the codes and conventions operative within the Western tradition of image making. The form taken by the remainder of this chapter may be best understood by recalling the historical depth model (*see* Fig. 2, p. 28). We will commence by examining the conventions that are present at the bottom-most levels and then gradually move upwards towards 'the light of consciousness'.

The fundamentals of the image

Prepared fields

When we make, or look at, a two-dimensional image it is remarkably easy to overlook the high level of conventionality that is at work and which structures and organises our ability to grasp what is seen. Usually what we are looking at will consist of an object which has a smooth, prepared surface and it will probably be something which has a set of regular, geometric boundaries. But as Meyer Schapiro[3] states:

> Such a field corresponds to nothing
> in nature or mental imagery where the
> phantoms of visual memory come up in a
> vague, unbounded world.[4]

We need only look at prehistoric cave art to realise that such 'prepared fields' have not always been thought as an essential foundation for image making. The cave painters of Lascaux painted their images upon unprepared surfaces which lacked boundaries. Not only this, the field of one execution was invaded by the painter superimposing another image on top of the first creating what appears, to our eyes, to be an anarchic palimpsest. It would appear that the completion of a work 'exhausted' its function and re-activated the field for a later effort. If we recall our earlier remarks (in chapt. 3, p. 60) concerning the importance of intermediate technologies to the execution of a work it should be clear that numerous such technologies were instrumental in making available such smooth surfaces onto which visual signs could be placed. For example, polished tools, pottery, the surface of dwellings, along with later, more complex materials such as woven fibres and papyrus. It seems likely that the bulk of such inscriptions were inseparable from the more general range of artifacts produced within a culture and as such, the fields onto which they were placed were intimately bound up with the forms such artifacts took.

Together with such prepared surfaces other features of the

image began to appear. The uniformity of the colour of the surface/background, something fundamental to our assumptions about the transparency of the picture plane. This was accompanied by the emergence of a bounded and discrete space, that is a precise and defined space which becomes 'specialised' for the reception of visual markings and signs. This does not have to be either regular or geometric, but could accommodate itself to a multiplicity of situations such as archways or the shape of the artifact being used. The appearance of precise boundaries, or edges, to the picture space is important for the representation of space and spatial relations for, without such boundaries, it is difficult to see how the particular elements of an image could ever be interpreted in spatial terms — the very term 'unbounded' implies precisely the absence of a spatial dimension. Even the emergence of a set of clear boundaries to the *depictive space* does not automatically guarantee an homogeneity of function to the area so enclosed. Certainly in some visual traditions this did follow, but within other traditions such as the Chinese the bounded space is seen as consisting of differential registers. Here it was legitimate for successive owners to write comments within the 'dead' space of the background. Even in the West elements of differential space are present in that it is permissible for artists to place their signatures in such a way as to overlay the depiction.

Frames and edges
We have an expectation that two-dimensional images will be bounded by a regular edge (margin) and in many instances a frame as well. Schapiro argues that such a convention is a relatively late phenomenon and was preceded by a number of earlier forms. The horizontal base line appears first and doubles up as the bottom of the image and as a grounding line which acts as a support for the figurative elements. Here the image consists of a number of horizontal bands which are often meant to represent the sequence of events within a narrative (*see* ill. 22). It was only later that the vertical margins of the field became pronounced and joined up with the horizontal margins to form 'an homogenous enclosure like a city wall'. The frame is a much later development and usually acts like a window frame, enclosing and focusing the viewer's gaze onto the scene which unfolds within its boundaries. Such a device places the frame within the space of the viewer and marks the point where 'real space' ends and represented space begins. The

22. The creation of Adam and Eve and their expulsion from the Garden of Eden. From the Moutier-Grandval Bible, Tours, 834-843 AD (British Library)

convention of constructing frames out of precious materials clearly signals the image as being a precious object, but it can also signify depictive intensity, the place where something special or extraordinary is taking place.

We might say that the modern concept of the frame is that of a regular enclosure isolating the field of representation from the surrounding surfaces, and marking the area in which the conventions of the image became operative.

Figure and field

It has long been known that *where* one places a pictorial element within a bounded field can dramatically affect the meaning which that element has — the area bounded by the frame is not all of a piece, that is it is not a neutral field of homogeneous possibilities. A mark in the top left corner of a pictorial field is not the same as an identical mark in the bottom right corner. Schapiro identifies five co-ordinates that should be considered when examining the differential effects generated by field relations. These are

broad, narrow
upper, lower
central, peripheral
left, right
corners and rest of the space

The degree to which these effects are created by the force of conventionality or by universal perceptual pre-dispositions is unknown. Whatever the causes, the effects can be palpable. Two illustrations will suffice here.

In terms of upper and lower, a regular bounded frame would appear to carry within it strong echoes from our experience of everyday space. The bottom of the picture is assumed to be lower in space (nearer the ground) than the upper portion. When novel viewing points are introduced or an image is placed in an 'unusual' situation much of this spatial ordering can be sent spinning (*see* ill. 23). Schapiro uses the example of a portrait by Munch (*see* ill. 24). In this image, Schapiro claims that by placing the figure to one side, away from the centre, the artist is able to suggest a host of psychological properties to his subject. Qualities like displacement, anomie, spiritual tension, are all increased by the figure being placed to one side of the image. At the same time the spatial and spiritual emptiness surrounding the figure is better signified by the empty space stretching away to its left.

Much more could be written about these deep structures of image organisation. For now we can say that these constitute a set of basic building blocks upon which rests the more complex and specific codes and conventions of image production. Even at this

23. Giovanni Battista Tiepolo: ceiling painting, the Holy House of Loreto, 1745 (Archivi Aldinari)

level it is clear that the distinctiveness of visual imagery derives as much from the relations between the various elements of an image as it does from the mere presence of coded units. It should also be clear that such relationships display very long continuities suggesting that they have histories which violate the 'periodisations' which derive from changes happening in the more labile levels

24. Edvard Munch: *Melancholy* 1891-92
(Munch Museet, Oslo)

closer to the surface. Nevertheless, these are codes and conventions which are integral to our ways of making visual images and as such are constantly being re-activated and re-worked. They are *encodings*, albeit at a very deep level.

Ways of depicting

The next level of conventionality to be considered rests upon the codes and conventions which relate to the ways in which the visual marks stand-in-for other things. We are now moving 'upwards' in terms of our depth model. A number of conceptual difficulties which this level presents need first to be outlined.

When surveying the variations in the ways of making Art in the Western tradition it is essential to attempt to group them into very broad categories of similarity. But the way such groupings are undertaken runs the risk of imparting to these purely descriptive categories some form of developmental schema such as A gives rise to B gives rise to C, with C being seen as the latest and therefore most 'advanced' mode of making Art. To tabulate the types of Art making that have existed and not speculate upon the relationships that exist between them rules out the possibility of ever considering how these differ. This difficulty is compounded in cultures with a lengthy period of literacy — a set of 'earlier stages'. Here the temptation is always to see the present as emerging out of one definition of civilisation and to incorporate previous epochs into a story about its emergence.

One of the ways in which we might approach the term 'ways of depicting' would be to return to Peirce's typology of signs, particularly to his distinction between iconic and symbolic signs. Undoubtedly certain images display more of the features of the icon than the symbol, or vice versa. The different types of sign relationship identified by Peirce may in fact undergo differential degrees of dispersal within a culture's general assumptions about what visual images are. One of these types of sign relationship will be privileged at the expense of the other — achieving a degree of dominance within that culture's ways of depicting (or, what is more likely, they will be found to occur in differential mixes). I think it is possible to push this assertion further and say that the Art of particular historical periods may be characterised by the ways in which these two sign relationships are combined. To back this up I will compare two ways of depicting in which it is possible to detect one of these sign relationships in a clear position of dominance.

The iconic rules

Every student of Art History knows of the Renaissance. This 'revolution' is generally associated with the idea that this was the *moment* when the archaic ways of visual representation gave way to, or were supplemented by, that 'thing' called *perspective*. Undoubtedly, something radical happened to the way European Art was produced; a profound shift occurred in the conventions governing the production of that Art. It started to do and be something unique to the West of the period. What was unique was the degree of intensity with which these conventions were applied to the making of images. Again it must be emphasised that there was not a total displacement of other ways of depicting, nor did it mean that certain functions of these other visual modes were not carried on within the new set of conventions.

One way of conceiving this shift is to see it as a gradual rise to dominance of the iconic visual sign. This drive towards iconic dominance is a confluence of two new conventional priorities within the making of images. It is their combinations which mark off this way of depicting as a radical shift. The two strands are *the mimetic*; that is the desire to make visual images with a high degree of resemblance between the visual signs and the objects they stand in for (Peirce's icon). This was joined to the conventions of perspective where the image as a whole was required to depict in two-dimensions, objects and their relations in physical space (three dimensions). The iconic tendency in the Art of the European Renaissance can then be seen as a double move in the re-organisation of the visual image. The first intensifies the degree of resemblance between the visual sign and the thing it stands in for, but as well as this micro-level, there is the macro-level where the whole image was regarded as being in a relationship of resemblance to the spatial relationships among the elements depicted.

It is important to stress that the appearance of mimesis and perspective does not necessarily mean that we are propelled immediately into the modern world. For instance, both sets of conventions were perfectly capable of being used to depict decidedly 'unmodern' worlds (*see* ill. 25). What does happen, however, is that certain conventions of image making come into being and remain in dominance until the threshold (and beyond) of the Modern period. What is the nature of this 'new' way of depicting? Perhaps its most distinctive feature is that the image starts to approximate to the model of theatre, with the illusionary space of the depiction approaching that of a stage set. Thus the plane of the picture becomes transparent rather like the fourth wall of a stage set which faces outwards to the audience. This enables the eyes of the viewer to travel into the illusionary depth which stretches back from the picture plane to the vanishing point. Within this space the viewer is able to observe the action depicted rather like someone seated in front of a stage watching a play. Because the mimetic strand crosses the conventions of perspective (stage-set model) the frequency of symbolic signs begins to recede. What is now stressed is a priority for depicting objects which rests on being able to translate visual perceptions into pictorial marks. For instance, the magnitude of figures within the image is determined according to their supposed physical distance from the picture plane or according to their relative positions *vis à vis* one another in the illusionary depth of the image. This lessened the opportunities to utilise symbolic visual signs and presented artists with a number of problems. Symbolic ways of depicting are very efficient at representing less concrete realities such as political significance, social standing, or

25. Matthias Grünewald: Isenheim Altar *The Temptation of Saint Anthony*
*c.*1512-15 (Musée d'Unterlinden-Colmar)

spiritual states. Since these were still important themes for Art, ways of indicating such qualities had to be devised without violating the mimetic and conventions of perspective. Artists resorted to

26. Leonard Beck. *Saint George Fighting the Dragon* c.1515
(Kunsthistoriches Museum, Vienna)

using insignia, costume, posture, gestures or particular placements
within the bounded fields of the images. In order to be able to perform its religious and social functions the image employed iconic
representations of conventional symbols which were operative in
the daily life of the society.

Another difficulty caused by the rise to dominance of an iconic
mode of depiction was that of how to represent the passage of
time. Because of the instantaneous nature of the iconic visual sign

various devices were used to solve this problem. Visual imagery involved a complex set of supplementary conventions to enable the passage of time to be marked. For instance the organisation of the action or events within a scene in such a way that 'before' and 'after' states could be imagined by the viewer. In the example shown above (*see* ill. 26), the artist has blocked out the overall space within the frame into a number of sequential scenes. The result of all such devices is paradoxical in that as the image strove to stand in more and more for what it desired to represent — a perfect resemblance — the more the presence of the viewer, in the form of their look, was being woven into the organisation of the image.

Throughout this examination of the iconic mode of depiction I have stressed that we rarely, if at all, encounter them in a pure state. Rather the iconic and symbolic modes resemble a series of irregular layers sedimented one on top of the other. Many types of visual imagery ignore the conventions of the mimetic-perspectival system and appear closer to the symbolic mode. The illustrations accompanying children's literature, cartoons and comics obviously reside within very different sign systems. Modern advertising appears to be able to mix up these two systems in some bizarre ways — size equals importance, colour equals emotional state, and inanimate objects speak. None of this seems to cause us much difficulty in comprehension mainly because we are always inhabiting a number of visual sign systems simultaneously.

The symbolic sign

One of the difficulties experienced by individuals brought up within the mimetic-perspectival conventions of image making so dominant in the West is that we have difficulty in designating 'other' systems in terms other than negative ones. We constantly refer to *non-realistic* Art, or *non-naturalistic* and *non-figurative* ways of depicting, as if the positive of these terms — realistic, naturalistic, figurative — were the accepted norm and all other systems, eccentric deviations. (For instance, what does the prefix 'non' signify in the list?) The dominance of the iconic mode can be gauged by the number of occasions you have heard the question, 'What is it?' directed at a work of Art. There are, however, two examples of visual sign systems which do not exhibit iconic dominance, but in different ways move towards a utilisation of systems much closer to the symbolic mode. These are the Art of tribal peoples — the Art that is often described by the perjorative term 'Primitive Art' — and that of the Modern period — that is 'Modern Art'.

Recall the features of *the symbolic visual sign* because we will see that these two ways of depicting inflect the visual sign in different ways. (Remember the symbolic sign is one where the relationship between the 'signifier' — the physical marks — and the object it stands in for is an 'arbitrary relationship'; the relationship between the signifier/object and the viewer of the sign is governed solely by a convention.)

Anthropologists specialising in the study of the Art of tribal peoples point to two unusual features for Westerners.[5] Firstly, their visual systems appear to be very low on what we would regard as 'life like' depictions or renderings, but also they lack what we would term Abstract Art. These absences point to a way of depicting that is very different to those we are familiar with; these are cultures whose visual sign systems are based on organising principles or conventions different from the mimetic-perspectival system of post-Rennaissance Art *and* that Art which is referred to as *Modern*. This difference lies in the fact that the Visual Art of such people is overwhelmingly a social phemonena with a sacred significance. This collective dimension enters into and shapes the very forms of Art itself. It is the primacy of the social function of their sign making that explains the very low level of 'life-like' representations. The role of their Art is to embody the *social meaning* of a figure, animal, or object rather than rendering what it looks like. So a chief will be identifiable by the incorporation into the image of a set of collectively held symbols, not by the depiction of individual physiognomic features. Again we need to stress that we are speaking here of a tendency towards the dominance of a particular type of sign, not its absolute presence. The representations of animals and objects within such types of Art often contain observations of extraordinary accuracy based upon highly detailed observation, but they are then deployed within the framework of a collective symbol system.

If the priority of much tribal Art is to foreground and embody the social attributions of the object no 'exaggeration' or 'distortion' is ignored to achieve this end. Figures of gods may be depicted with glaring eyes and gaping mouths perfectly encapsulating both their sacred status and the respect in which they are held. Other figures may emphasise the sexual organs as a token of their virility and power. We might say that there is a general disregard of, or indifference towards the conventions of the mimetic-perspectival system because the tribal artist is treading a different path and producing beneath a different set of imperatives, uppermost of which is a desire to symbolise the social relationships between the members of the group and their physical and spiritual environment. Proportion in such contexts means *social proportion.*

The anthropologist, Raymond Firth,[6] locates the difference between the tribal ways of depicting and those of the Western tradition in the nature of the types of visual signs which are being deployed. Tribal art is dominated by a *collectively held* set of symbols, that is signs which rest upon a cultural knowledge (conventions) for their comprehension rather than a perceptual association. As such it is only through an understanding of the myths and general way of life of a people that we can enter into the meanings carried by such symbols. It also follows that the symbolism of tribal art is the common property of its producers and its audience; the conventions governing the meaning of the symbols constantly circulates amongst the members of the group; one rarely encounters a purely private symbolism. Such visual symbols are important *emblems* which help to mark the group as a unit whilst at the same time differentiating it from other groups. In such situations it is the presence of the symbol itself which is vital — questions of 'naturalistic depiction' being irrelevant. Firth illustrates this by way of an example taken from the Art of the Indians of British Columbia in Canada:

> The beaver, as one group emblem, is represented on totem poles, tobacco pipes, and many other objects. The presence of this animal may be difficult to identify in a design, since the artist is apt to dissect the subject and distribute the parts around the field without regard to their normal anatomical relations. Or he portrays merely some of them, as crucial indices. So it is sufficient, if the figure has a short fat tail with cross-hatched markings on it, to recognize it as a beaver. Again much of the beaver's activity is concerned with timber, so if a stick is held by the figure in the design, that also signifies a beaver. Moreover, the beaver may be given a human face, in token of its human affiliations. Here, then, is a complex piece of symbolic art, in which a carved representation of a nose, teeth, a tail, or a stick, symbolizes an animal; the animal symbolizes a human group; and this relation is itself symbolized by depicting the animal with a human face.[7]

27. Haida Indian: Wooden bowl shaped as a bear. N.d.
(Milwaukee Public Museum)

Where such sign systems differ from the mimetic-perspectival system is that they do not share the assumptions of the latter that objects can exist independently of the sign/symbol maker and the group to which they belong. By this I mean there is an assumption within the mimetic-perspectival system that the net thrown over objects by the conventions of perspective are somehow 'objective'. By translating the co-ordinates established by this grid into pictorial marks one is able to produce a representation of the 'thing' as it really is. That is, a representation independent of its depicter and its viewer. The beaver, in the example presented by Firth, is always a significant thing, the signs of which aim to embody this significance as vividly as possible (*see* ill. 27).

The Modernist symbol[7]

Although the Modernist movement in the Visual Arts has consistently seen the Art of tribal peoples as being closer in spirit to its imperatives than the Art of the post-Renaissance period, an examination of the ways in which it has exploited the symbolic visual sign reveals that it, in fact, heads off in directions very different to those of tribal Art. What it does do (some might say obsessively) is to put into doubt Art's ability to stand in for something else.

We may differentiate the Modernist way of depicting in two general ways. In terms of the conventions of the mimetic-perspectival system, Modernist Art has moved away from seeing the Art work in purely iconic terms, thus putting a question mark behind the very words we use; a picture of . . .?; an image of . . .?;

a representation of . . .? Whenever and wherever the word 'of' occurs in those sentences, it has been one of the priorities of Modernist Art to disturb our easy transition across its assumptions. Modernist Art vociferously disputes the status to be assigned to the overall image field, and so undermines the whole panoply of 'standing-in-for' that the European visual tradition rested upon. In contrast to tribal Art, or better still, systems of Art which rest upon a high level of shared and conventional symbolism, Modernist Art has deliberately (and sometimes accidentally) eschewed the collective, the shared, and the conventional in favour of the individual, the private and 'the new' in terms of the types of visual sign it has resorted to. In Modernist Art what happened was not the emergence of a totally unified and coherent way of depicting, rather a continuing oscillation *between* a variegated set of axes.

The first of these Modernist axes of movement is the tension between the work of Art as a referential sign, that is a sign that stands in for something (both as icon and symbol) and the work of Art as an autonomous, non-referential object. Even a cursory perusal of Modernist Art will reveal that its mimetic function persists with varying degrees of intensity — we can still 'recognise' objects in the works. What does happen though is that in some works the 'pointing to' function recedes dramatically with work aspiring to the status of absolute non-referentiality (for example, Suprematist painting) or attempting to become 'objects amongst other objects'. In certain of Mondrian's grid paintings the lines of the grid stop just short of the edge. Some critics have interpreted this as a desire on Mondrian's part to stop the viewer seeing the boundaries of the field as approximating to a window with the assumption that the grid-lines continue out of sight. Such a device may be attempting to mark these works as pure non-referential objects, things in their own right. If the Art of the post-Renaissance was a kind of visual drawbridge lowered out onto the world, Modernist Art would pull the drawbridge up and point to the 'objecthood' of the very plane that the lowering of the drawbridge allowed to vanish.

The disappearance of a shared symbol system in Modernist Visual Arts, threw the traditional role of Art as a system of objective signs mediating between the members of a collective into crisis. Art became characterised by the proliferation of private symbols — or rather marks with highly localised meanings and this threw the relationship between producer and viewer into confusion. What the meaning of a particular work was and where it was to be located − in the producer or in the viewer − became increasingly important factors in the game of Modernist Art. The absence of any generalised set of conventions about the status of the artistic sign has been at the back of the continuing and acrimonious skirmishes that have broken out between the producers and the consumers of Modernist Art over the question of 'What is it?'

This ambiguity at the centre of Modernist Art about the appropriate conventions to bring to bear on the work can been seen in the tension between the aesthetic function of the work and its other functions. One of the characteristics of the visual sign that we will explore later in this book is its ability to be grasped in terms of its mimetic qualities and its aesthetic qualities simultaneously and, the economy with which these two aspects can be combined within a visual sign is a source of great pleasure. Towards the end of the 19th century, particularly in the *l'art pour l'art* movement the aesthetic aspect of the artistic sign began to be privileged over its referential aspect. The Modern Movement pushed this even further producing works which aimed to purge the artistic sign of all of its non-aesthetic functions. The 'pure' forms of geometric abstraction, the 'non-objective' colours and shapes of Kandinsky were seen as ends, not means. They were regarded as distillations of the aesthetic properties of the artistic sign and therefore somehow 'purer' embodiments of the essence Art. Despite the desire on the part of artists to make their work approximate to the status of music, the viewers of Art have stubbornly held to a view of the visual sign as a dual entity − something which is both aesthetic *and* referential.

Where the iconic way of depicting is in dominance − for instance in the mimetic-perspectival sign system − the materiality of the image tends to disappear in order for the iconic illusion to work to its greatest effect. One of the paradoxes of the great tradition of European oil painting is that it achieves it greatest successes to the extent that it is able to make the very medium of its depiction disappear, namely the paint. Within the Modernist subversion of the iconic processes of the image two strategies have been adopted to highlight the materiality of the visual sign. The first found its most coherent expression in the writings of the USA critic, Clement Greenberg. This argument was that the Arts, in order to fulfil most fully their 'essence', had to discover and isolate what it was that was unique to their particular medium. Greenberg, in his meditations upon painting, decided that it was flatness and the delimitation of flatness together with the paint and its support (the canvas) which constituted the 'essence' of painting. The artists who concurred with his philosophy then set out to concern themselves with these 'essential' dimensions and this in turn lead to an increasing emphasis upon the *materiality* of marks, paint and the supports upon which they rested. The other strategy was to draw attention to the objectness of the Art work by a series of internal oscillations between 'prepared' material and 'untreated' objects. In this way the viewer is switched across a set of differential visual signs which, in combination, stop the iconic illusion operating. For example, the collages of Kurt Schwitters where painted and 'found' elements are included within a common field.

The final axis of Modernist Art is that strand of work that sets out to explore the very nature of the line that separates the artistic sign, or work, from the non-artistic. This is part of a much larger desire on the part of Modernist artists to grasp the foundations upon which their practice and its products rest. Two very different examples will suffice here. The Belgian artist René Magritte painted a highly realistic image of a tobacco pipe beneath which he placed the sentence 'Ceci n'est pas une pipe'. In doing this he draws our attention to our continuing propensity to misrecognise the sign of an object for the thing itself. Marcel Duchamp, master of the ironic gesture, was partial to the strategy of putting non-Art objects such as bottle racks and urinals into situations where they appeared to take on the status of Art. He would then stand back and enjoy the distress and confusions which his serious humour had caused.

The major lesson to be gleaned from this discussion is that these general ways of depicting are highly conventionalised (rule-bound) sign systems which rest upon differential sets of priorities governing what it is that the users of such systems imagine to be the function that such systems should accomplish. More often than not these deep levels are only partially 'known', if at all, by their users, but in this they are no different from all the other 'frames of reference' that we employ in order to exist in a world that is meaningful.

Genres

So far in our discussion of the coded nature of the image we have been examining bodies of conventions which help form what we might call *species* of images. But as long ago as Aristotle it has been recognised that Art has tended to form itself into *families*, where relations of similarity can be detected between artistic kinfolk. It is in film that such groupings are most well known with such divisions as the western, the thriller, the romantic comedy or the musical. A similar phenomenon can be detected in the Visual Arts where certain picture types emerge and persist, sometimes for centuries. So we have landscapes, still life, flower pictures, portraits, the nude and historical painting, to list just a few of the most well known. The name given to such picture families is *genre*, and whilst it is often thought that the Art of the twentieth century has seen the collapse of such picture types, it is remarkable how the traditional groupings have persisted — albeit in altered form — and how new genres have arisen. For instance, that most singular and notorious 'ism' of Modern Art, Cubism, was crossed by four traditional painting genres — still life, portraiture, landscape, and the nude. What are genres in the Visual Arts and how do they operate at the levels of production and coding? In terms of their overall placement they are perhaps best thought of as constituting the next level of conventionality above the ways of depicting. Whilst it is true to say that they may be seen as subgroupings within ways of depicting, they are not strictly confined within these boundaries. As we have already mentioned in relation to Cubism they can survive some very profound paradigm shifts in those conventions, only to emerge re-invigorated. As a descriptive term, genre points to three general characteristics

Similarity
Persistence
Specialisation

Similarity
At it most obvious level genre points to the fact that two or more visual images display certain similar features. It is a term then that enables us to think and talk about what is the same or similar within a particular set of Art works. When we use a generic label, such as 'landscape' or 'still life', it will normally engender in the mind of the reader a set of associations as to what type of image is being referred to. Such associations will, in all probability, contain information about the subject matter of the images, but it will also carry within it suggestions as to how that subject matter is dealt with. The complex debates about what genres are, either at a

general level, or in terms of a particular genre, always attempt to knit these two aspects together. Both are essential for a genre to be adequately defined.

Persistence

Given that it is possible to establish sameness or similarity amongst a body of imagery, genre must also be able to deal with the persistence of such similarity over time. There can never be a genre of one image, there must always be a recurrence of similarity. For instance, within the tradition of Western Art, the still life spans a period from the 15th century through Cubism to the present day.

This means that genres always have a history and given enough evidence, it is possible to see them coming into being, stabilising (persisting) and in some instances dying out or undergoing an internal transformation into a different genre. Why and how genres do this is only partially understood. It is possible for some genres to emerge from, live through and live out wildly differing social conditions or historical epochs. During the 19th century we find the genre of the nude increasingly focusing upon the body of the woman. The male body as a 'fit' topic becomes rarer and rarer, confined to the productions of the life class and the student sketch. On the other hand some visual genres can come and go like mayflies, suddenly enjoying immense popularity and vanishing just as quickly. It is possible that at any moment there may be a number of genres in existence some ascending others in decline. These generic ebbs and flows occur independently of the conscious choices made by individual artists and while they may make conscious decisions about which genre is the appropriate one to work with, the rise, fall and persistence of each genre appears to have an existence independent of such individual decisions.

I have generally eschewed matters of aesthetic value in this book but it has to be raised at this point because the nature of genres unsettles many of the Modernist assumptions held about value in Art. We Moderns tend to see the best Art as that which breaks with convention and regularity and we prize Art that 'clears new ground.' However, a great deal of the Art of the past which we value, is highly genericised. A landscape by Nicolas Poussin (1594-1665), an interior by Jan Vermeer (1632-75), a portrait by Velasquez (1599-1660) are all supreme examples of particular painting genres. The greatness of such works comes from a variety of sources; they may be the best example of a genre, they may have been works which entered an ailing genre and completely re-enlivened it, or they may even appear to establish a genre in a single stroke such that the artists who followed could only vary a formula established by the founding image. For centuries genre was the normal operating condition of Western Art.

Specialisation

It would appear to be a relatively easy task to identify a genre. The very labels portraiture, the nude, still life, landscape, and other classifications suggest bodies of work that can be grouped together according to their choices of subject matter. They are genres because they specialise in depicting particular objects, or sets of objects from the real world or the world of the imagination. Such a rationale certainly gets us moving, but we should remember that there has always been an ancillary set of ideas about genres, namely that genre was also concerned with *how* a particular subject matter was to appear and what it was that that content meant. We might say the titles of painting genres were a set of agreements about what a particular genre 'was about'. With the establishment of Royal Academies of Art in 18th-century Europe there also arose an hierarchy of genres which ranked them in terms of their seriousness and philosophical ambition. History painting was regarded as the greatest test that a painter could undertake both in terms of the skills demanded by the topic but also by the profundity of its meaning. Still life, however, was regarded as a minor genre.

Depicting the land or the countryside was not simply a matter of presenting a view of nature in any way one felt, because as a painting genre, landscape was seen as a vehicle through which certain visions of perfection and harmony could be made manifest. For Poussin landscape was the setting for, and an embodiment of Arcadia, the rural paradise. For Jean Antoine Watteau (1684-1721), landscape became a setting in which an aristocratic fantasy of unending pleasure and delight could unfold. For the Romantic painters of the late 18th and early 19th century landscape could become a way of representing the harmony of an imaginary pre-industrial way of life (Samuel Palmer, 1789-1854) or of apocalyptic dreams of destruction and transcendence (John Martin, 1805-1881). In the 20th century landscape has often been tied to nationalism and regionalism where, as an antidote to the homogenised agglomerations of the global village, nations and regions have struggled to construct a sense of difference and distinctness. In such movements landscape has been seen as a way of representing those unique qualities in an intense manner. Thus the genre of landscape has had a shifting set of significances and in each instance this can be characterised as both a depiction of nature and a process of idealisation, but the nature of this idealisation can and has varied immensely. It is precisely this ability of genres to drift across a range of meanings that enables them to outlive the immediate circumstances of their appearance.

Style

We are now approaching the uppermost levels of coding and conventionality. Our next level, *style*[8] may be thought of as marking the threshold between the conscious and unconscious elements within the image. It is one of the areas where artists begin to formulate for themselves the operations of coding. This is borne out in the statements which artists make about their work and *modus operandii* where we find them shuttling back and forth across this threshold as the marks being made begin to suggest a meaning and significance that can only fleetingly be grasped.

Style then can denote the overall pattern of regularities within an image, or style is the form in which the image appears, the concrete patterns within the marks that are made on the image surface. These idiosyncrasies of depiction can be detected *within* the work of a single artist or *between* the works of a number of practitioners. Some Art Historians claim that nations or whole historical periods can exhibit such stylistic patterns, but the evidence for such claims remains dubious. One example will serve here.

Certain Expressionist artists of the early 20th century exhibited a distinctive stylistic feature in their work. The device is the thick, black outline used to 'rough in' the body or the face of the figure. One commentator has described this feature in the image by Georges Rouault (ill. 28) in the following way:

> Painted with an almost frantic brushstroke the figure is outlined in heavy black against the background of the brothel.[9]

He then goes on to provide the viewer with the significance that such marks were supposed to have:

> They [Expressionist artists] searched for affirmation in various forms of primitive art, hoping to regain the emotional impact and . . . power of the iconic object.[10]

28. Georges Rouault: *Odalisque* 1907
(Oeffentliche Kunstsammlung Basel Kunstmuseum)

First the description of the stylistic element − in this case the 'frantic' brushstroke and the 'heavy, black outline' − and then its meaning − it is more emotional, redolent of the 'primitive' and the authentic. It is the general acceptance of this intrepretative move that enables such marks, or pictorial devices, to acquire a particular meaning. In this sense style refers to those elements within an image which the passage of time reveals to have been particular to one artist or which were shared by a number of artists within a particular period. The important point is that they subsequently reveal themselves as conventional signs, not elements with a necessary connection to their meanings at the time. So style is the last point of conventionality before it becomes fashion. In some cases it can overlap with fashion and thereby becomes a sign which captures the quintessence of that period.

The artist

We have reached the uppermost level of our shaft, where the makers of the works live, produce and make their sets of choices about what form the work should take. In a way our depth model, whilst a useful analytical device is misleading in that it implies that the codes and conventions we have been describing are in the past buried and invisible to the individual attempting to produce a satisfactory work. A better way to conceive of this final level is as a place to be occupied when production is commenced. Rather than an open field of operation, the place of making a symbolic object is a shaped field, a situation in which there are both determining elements and elements which present the maker with a set of opportunities. It is a place where past, present and future collide and intersect. Every instance of Art making crosses and re-activates this enormous historical, but shifting, deposit of codes and conventions that we call tradition. How a particular artist chooses to act within these codes can never be determined before-hand — in that sense Art Theory is very low on prediction. Some may prefer to remain within certain types of conventions, hence the generic families of imagery and broad stylistic regularities. The Art produced by adhering to tradition will manifest a high degree of conventionalism; what is more, it may do this willingly, happy to remain loyal to forms that have persisted for centuries. Other artists may operate with a different set of priorities, often sensing that what they are doing is extending the versatility of a medium by up-ending the traditional codes and conventions. What I have attempted to show in this chapter is that no matter where one places oneself in the enormous range of possibilities confronting the contemporary artist, failure to play the game according to some type of rules is the one possibility that is absent.

1   Peirce's references to signs are scattered through his voluminous writings, C. S. Peirce *Collected Papers* (8 vols) Charles Hartshorne, Paul Weiss, and Arthur W. Burks (eds), Harvard: Harvard University Press, 1931-1958.

2   C. S. Peirce *Collected Papers* vol. 2, para. 228.

3   In this section I have drawn on Meyer Schapiro 'On Some Problems in the Semiotics of Visual Art: Field and Vehicle in Image Signs in *Semiotica* Thomas Sebeok (ed.), vol. I, The Hague: Mouton, 1969, pp. 223-42.

4   *Ibid.* p. 223.

5   In this section I have drawn upon Raymond Firth *Elements of Social Organization* London: Watts, 1951. *See especially* ch. 5 'The Social Framework of Primitive Art' pp. 155-82.

6   Firth *ibid.* p. 178.

7   In this section I have drawn upon the discussion of Jan Mukarovsky's writings on Modernist Art in Thomas G. Winner 'On the relation of verbal and non-verbal art in early Prague Semiotics: Jan Mukarovsky' in *The Sign: Semiotics around the World* R. W. Bailey, L. Matejka, and P. Steiner (eds), Ann Arbor: Michigan Slavic Publications, 1978, pp. 227-37.

8   My use of the term style, in this context, is rather personal. The reader should be aware that in Art History the term has a long and complex development. The most useful summaries are: Judith Genova 'The Significance of Style in *Journal of Aesthetics and Art Criticism* vol. 37, 1978, pp. 315-24; Ernst Gombrich *Art and Illusion* London: Phaidon, 1962. *See especially* 'Introduction: the Riddle of Style'; also Meyer Schapiro 'Style' in *Anthropology Today* A. L. Kroeber (ed.), Chicago: University of Chicago, 1953,
    pp. 278-303.

5
The work of Art as commodity

In 1987 Vincent van Gogh's painting *The Sunflowers* was bought by the Japanese corporation Yasuda for $55 million. How is it that a physical object measuring 91 cms by 72 cms and consisting of canvas and oil paint is able to acquire such extraordinary economic value? Clearly it has nothing to do with the value of the materials that it is made of, or the value of the labour which the painter Van Gogh expended in its production. Although the myth that Van Gogh did not sell any of his work is not correct, he was certainly not a 'successful' artist by any reasonable measure. We might want to claim that the economic value of this is a reflection of its aesthetic value, but here again there are difficulties in explaining why Van Gogh would appear to be so much better a painter than other artists whose work fetches nowhere near these extraordinary amounts. To answer these questions we need to consider that dimension of the Art object which relates to its life as an economic value or a commodity.

We will begin our examination at Box I (p. 45), with the artist-producer. Artists in contemporary society rarely avail themselves of naturally occurring materials but are dependent upon inter-mediate technologies to provide the materials which are sub-sequently utilised to construct the Art object. That is the 'raw materials' of Art and the work of the artist rest upon other systems of work and production to provide them with their 'raw materials'. In order to clarify the nature of the work of Art as an economic value, or commodity we need, at this point, to make the distinction between *work* and *labour*. Work may be defined as the physical and mental processes which are required to transform one set of materials into a finished product. Labour refers to the economic structures which put a price upon the quantity and quality of any particular kind of work. For artistic production to commence, the artist has to use materials that have been produced by different sets of work, for example, pigments, canvas, paper, pencils. But, in order to acquire such materials they must have a sum of money on hand — they are not free — because in order for them to be produced the manufacturers of these materials have had, among other costs, to pay for the labour of their workers. So even before artistic production commences the artist-producer is confronted by the necessity of having some type of financial resource in order to begin.

As well as access to materials an artist still needs to eat, sleep and move about in the world. There is a pressing need 'to keep body and soul together' in order to stay alive and continue to function. When the work is in progress additional funds have to be expended in order to maintain (re-produce) these conditions which make production possible.

The final component of Art production — the visual codes out of which the work emerges — might appear to be the element most free of financial considerations, but even here we encounter a hidden cost. As we have already seen, the training of artists is a long and complex process which today is normally undertaken within institutions that are equivalent to universities. (In a study conducted on tertiary education in Australia it was found that the cost of educating a student to the level of Bachelor of Fine Arts in 1979 was $3,575 per annum.) One of the most important aspects of this training is that of inducting the student into the particular traditions (the visual codes) which are in circulation within that country. Even after this process of training is officially completed continuing access to the visual codes of a particular tradition are crucial for the maturation of the adult artist and this means the ability to purchase books and visit exhibitions, galleries, and museums. The availability of, and open access to the codes requires that funds are also available in order to pay for the labour of gallery staff, conservators, transporters, and ancillary staff. In countries with strong Social Democratic traditions fine arts education and the cultural apparatus that surrounds it, are considered to be the responsiblity of the State therefore financial provision is supplied from the common purse. This still means that money in the form of a tax on the wages of labour has to be forth-coming. As we all know, in times of economic austerity the Arts can become an easy target for cuts, thus making access to the codes of a particular visual tradition increasingly difficult for practitioners.

We can summarise these basic conditions of artistic production in the following way: Any consideration of Art production must always bear these elementary conditions in mind because they clearly demonstrate that right from the moment of inception (and despite the myths and ideologies that surround notions of artistic creation), Art is embedded in intricate and collective networks of differential types of work, all of which are forms of labour and all of which therefore require considerable sums of money being expended in order to maintain the conditions of artistic production.

Use value and exchange value

We have established that certain fundamental conditions have to be met in order that the conditions for artistic production may come into being and be reproduced. These considerations enable us to insert the artist-producer and the work of artistic production into an economic structure but the object itself has not yet become a commodity, it does not yet have an economic value. Before we can examine how this takes place we need to make a further distinction between the *use value* of an object and its *exchange value*.

It is perhaps best to approach this particular complexity via a more mundane object and then see what this opens up for us in terms of the Art object. A can of soup has a clearly defined use value in that it is able to assuage — when consumed — the hunger experienced by an individual. We might also add that in highly sophisticated cultures, it may also have the additional ability to satisfy the desire of that individual for tomato soup — not minestrone or oxtail. Therefore the use value of a particular object (or service) is its ability to satisfy an identifiable need or desire present within the members of the group in which it is available. The *exchange value* of an object refers to a different dimension and may be initially grasped by the term *price*, or how much money will be required in order to buy the can of soup. However, as soon as the question of price is considered it will be seen that the exchange value of the soup is not simply about the amount of money required for its purchase, it is also to do with the system of equivalences that such a process of pricing establishes. So,

one can of soup = $1
one packet of nuts = $1
therefore one can of soup = one packet of nuts

The equivalence of soup and nuts takes place via the $1, so that we can say that the *exchange value* of the soup is a packet of nuts and vice versa. The result of this 'putting a price on its head' is that the economic value of an object can now be expressed in the form of a monetary value — if you have a dollar you can exchange it for a can of soup or a packet of nuts. It is this insertion into a set of equivalences that establishes an object as a commodity and it would also follow that there can never be just one commodity, it always needs another object with which it can be compared.

The use value of Art

The difficulty with comparing the use value of soup and of Art is that whilst the former can be easily related to the satisfaction of a tangible need called 'hunger', it is less easy to identify the need which Art satisfies without straying across into the land of hot air and vague generalisations. Rather than starting with a unified and contemporary category of Art *and then* ransacking the past for confirmatory examples, it is better to ask the simple and limited questions. For instance, 'What function (if any) did image X or object Y perform when it was produced?' This breaks the large and unmanageable question, into simpler and more easily resolvable ones. Three examples will suffice to establish my point. In each of these instances it is possible to identify a clear but different usage for each image. The first example (ill. 29) records the appearance and ownership of a particularly fine animal. In the second (ill. 30) a powerful political figure is depicted as being the author of a glorious victory. In the third (ill. 31) the appearance of a woman — as yet unseen — is conveyed to her future husband. In a sense the evidence is 'rigged' by selecting images where it is possible to identify a straightforward use for each of them. However, against this it is very difficult to answer in all honesty the general question, 'What is the use value of Art?' If, rather than looking in the past, we stay in the present, the range of uses to which Art is put still escapes generalisation. According to the particular encounter between image and viewer some Art may induce feelings of intense pleasure whilst others remain indifferent to it. Art objects may

29. Thomas Flintoff: *Henry F. Stone and his Durham Ox* 1887
(City of Ballarat Fine Art Gallery, Victoria)

30. Baron Gros: *Napoleon at Eylau* 1809 (Louvre, Paris)

31. Hans Holbein: *Anne of Cleves c.*1539-40
(National Portrait Gallery, London)

be used as forms of display, a way to indicate an individual's wealth or social status. It may act as a form of visual memory in much the same way as certain pieces of music. It can — but not necessarily does — act as a form of knowledge, as a way of fixing certain intimate and fleeting emotional states. It may act as a sign of national vigour or be pilloried as a sign of national decline. All these uses are possibilities and do happen, but I do not think that we can say that there is a single *use value* to which all Art conforms.

But if the use value of Art is both shifting and variegated, the exchange value is clearly something that we can all agree about simply because it manifests itself in an objective form, the price.

The exchange value of Art

All of us are familiar with the spectacular prices that major — and not so major — works by well known artists can fetch on the contemporary Art market. We are perhaps also familiar with newsreel footage taken in the international auction houses where the price of a Van Gogh or a Cézanne effortlessly reaches six figures and beyond. What is less clear is why this is so and how these symbolic objects are transformed into what amounts to bullion. In order to explain this it is necessary to insert these spectacular events into those much broader processes which transform the objects of artistic production into commodities, that is objects with exchange value.

Returning to the soup analogy: for the soup to realise its *use value* it must be able to reach the individual with a need for it and this means that there is some means of *distributing* the soup. Distribution of the soup creates a situation whereby it is possible for the individual to *buy* it (by exchanging money for it) and then satisfy their hunger by *consuming* it. If the soup remains in the warehouse or factory it is unable to realise both its use value and exchange value and if it isn't exchanged then it does not become *a commodity*.

At this fundamental level, Art is remarkably similar to soup but with one very important distinction. The Art object is a particular type of commodity, *a cultural commodity*. Of its three constituent dimensions, work, materials, visual codes, it is the last one, codes, that mark it off as being different from soup. The exchange value of the Art object is created when it becomes part of the generalised system that we might term *the traffic in codes*.

The distribution of Art commodities

The task of the Art distribution system is to ensure that the objects resulting from artistic production reach their prospective customers. Art objects enter into this 'traffic system' because most artists have to make use of intermediary institutions, or 'middlemen', who are called Art dealers and who own private galleries. The structures constituting the 'traffic lanes' of Art vary immensely from place to place, but most large cities in the Western world will have networks of such private Art galleries where it is possible to view and purchase works from the stable of artists which are attached to them. The distribution of Art has not always been organised in such a way. In western Europe when there was a distinct class of patrons such 'private' mechanisms were not necessary as artists and craftspeople were often permanently attached to the courts and households of aristocratic families.

We need to look at the types of relationship that hold between artist and dealer because it is here that we can locate the initial steps which transform an Art object into an Art commodity.

Very often a young artist will commence their public and economic careers by being invited to participate in a *Group Show*. This will consist of a few artists exhibiting a small number of works together with the hope that they may gain some initial recognition and perhaps even sell one of their works. The dealer will provide the premises, finance the catalogue, and provide food and drink for the guests at the opening. Through the distribution of invitations to the show they may try and ensure that it is noticed and is reviewed by journalists and critics. Of course, any works that are sold entail a percentage of their price being paid to the dealer.

The next stage beyond the group show is to be signed up by a private gallery. Again there are numerous ways of managing this relationship. The dealer may suggest that the artist work towards producing enough work for a one-person show (the same conditions as the group show will apply). Or, the dealer may draw up a contract with an artist to retain all the work they produce over a given period and in return will pay the artist a regular wage. The complexities of the various agreements between artist and private gallery generally increase in direct proportion to the success of the particular artist involved.

It is in the operations of the private galleries that two important processes get underway. The dealer/gallery owner is the initial *agent of distribution* for the Art work. It is they who attempt to 'place a work' and so it is here that we can locate the start of that process whereby the work begins to draw away from its immediate sphere of production. Galleries are always involved in a two-way traffic, attempting to sell work to customers, but also attempting to find customers for works. Galleries always have a number of collectors, institutions or museums which they will contact when they think a particularly appropriate work becomes available. So galleries not only operate for the producers of Art, they act on behalf of its consumers as well. It is in the gallery that the second crucial function is performed, namely the agreeing of the price to be asked for a work. It is here that we first encounter the transformation of the Art object into a commodity with an exchange value. Thus the private gallery is a crucial switching point where the Art object first enters into the system of exchange.

The price of Art

The most important question to be asked at this point is 'how is this price fixed?' Once again it is important to stress the *difference* between cultural commodities and 'normal' commodities in that the price of the Art object is not simply determined by forces operating at the point of production. The reasons for the differential nature of cultural-commodities lie in two directions. Firstly the point already made concerning the high code component and low use value of cultural commodities when compared with other commodities. Put simply this means that they are valuable in ways different from non-cultural commodities. The other difference lies in the particular nature of *Art labour.*

We are all familiar with the gasps of amazement, even the outbreaks of applause, which occur when a particularly high price is paid for a work of Art. I suspect that at the bottom of such exclamatory gestures lies, not necessarily moral disapproval, but rather bewilderment over the apparent disparity between the object and its newly acquired economic value. Such disparities seem to violate all of our commonsense ideas about the relation between an object and its price. A motor car is a very sophisticated piece of technology; it's big, and requires a considerable amount of time, materials and skill in order to be constructed. No matter how devastated we may be when informed of the purchasing price of a car, there is still the possibility of understanding *why* such an object costs that amount of money. This is not to say that such commonsense ideas are correct, simply that they are capable of producing a believable explanation. The difficulty with cultural commodities such as Art works is that none of these 'normal' schemas for evaluating price appear to work. A large work does not necessarily cost more that a small one, a work with obvious high degree of technical skill does not cost more that a sketch by a great master, whilst a forgery, which might look exactly like the original, is worthless.

Clearly the forces determining exchange value in Art are not the same as those operating in the realms of everyday economics.

If we begin by considering the nature of *artistic labour,* it would appear to be a relatively easy task to arrive at a 'guesstimate' for the price of work through simple addition. Price = cost of materials and hours spent on the work (the rate of for the job) +

extras (profit, outlay to intermediaries, inflation). But none of this really adds up to anything resembling the actual price and the real difficulty resides in that second figure, the labour of Art. From what we have already stated it should be clear that artists do not receive a wage based upon a fixed quantity of time expended at a fixed rate of money. The reason for this is that there are no longer any clearly defined *employers* of artists. In Eastern bloc countries with a high level of state control and administration of culture such a condition is approached. In the West, gallery owners may pay an artist an intermittent income, but this is not calculated in terms of the hours put in but rather as a way to ensure that the conditions for continuing production are reproduced. There is no agreed rate for the job. So the price of a new work of Art is determined not by the amount of labour expended but by other, more elusive factors.

Young artists exhibiting for the first time can expect to price their works at a very low level relative to the labour expended. It is hard to be more specific than this, other than to say that the exact price asked for a piece will vary against a general background of prices for this level of attainment. Dealers and artists visit galleries constantly and closely monitor the prices other artists are asking. If they are able to sell, then this is an indication of what the current market will bear and prices will be adjusted accordingly. There are, of course, many factors that will contribute to determining this 'generally agreed level'. The overall buoyancy of the national economy will be an important element. If there is a large amount of unused wealth floating around looking for a place to go, Art is very often the beneficiary. For example, in Australia during the early 1970s there was a boom in the price that minerals could command on the international markets and some of the surplus wealth generated during this period found its way into the Art market. There was an increase in the number of potential buyers and consequently many young artists were not only selling their works, but were selling them at relatively high prices. At other times when money is tight, wealth can quickly desert the unsure world of young artists and will flow instead into the purchase of 'safe' works, that is into works whose value is already well established. Another general factor is the way in which a society regards the importance of its Art and culture. If Art has a high profile, that is if it is reported, is talked about, and is underpinned by a significant number of interested consumers, then it will be able to command relatively higher prices than in societies where it is barely visible. Other patterns of distribution can be discerned. For instance, Art like many other cultural activities, is more highly concentrated in the metropolitan centres of a country than it is in the provinces. It is not just that there is more money in such centres, but also that there are more people with an avowed interest in the Arts and therefore more people likely to expend their wealth in purchasing Art objects. What holds within a single country can also hold on the international scene in that certain cities — New York, London, Tokyo — are regarded as being centres for the Art market. This does not necessarily ensure that all artists working in such cities can always command high prices for their works, but what it does mean is that recognition in any of these centres is likely to produce a greater income if and when it does occur.

The valorisation of the Art object

The picture building up is one in which the exchange value of the work of Art resembles much more closely the ebb and flows of stocks and shares than it does the price of something like our mythical can of soup. Just as that indeterminate quality 'market confidence' is so crucial to the rise and fall of the stock market, so *valorisation* of the Art work (and of the artist) is crucial to the rise and fall in the prices of Art. What is meant by the term 'valorisation' are the diverse mechanisms whereby a particular Art work becomes an object of interest and the subsequent transformation of such interest into economic value. If, for the moment, we remain with new works produced by relatively unknown artist, then 'interest' can issue from a number of sources. Just by appearing in a gallery signifies that 'someone-in-the-know' is sufficiently intrigued to consider it worthwhile displaying the work. A suggestion from a dealer that a piece may be worth purchasing may then result in a sale and sales of work are a sure sign that there is interest in that artist. One of the most frequent inquiries to be heard when artists get together is, 'Are you selling?' If the answer is 'yes', word will get round and others will become intrigued and notice taken of that individual's work. People may even try to get in on the ground floor by purchasing a work before prices get too high. Dealers, artists and potential buyers constantly scan the pages of newspapers, Art magazines, and so on, to see whose star is in the ascendant. Mention in such publications does not automatically guarantee a sale but, it is certainly one of the ways in which interest can begin to accumulate. Whenever an artist has a show, details of their career to date will be included in the catalogue and often this *curriculum vitae* will mention the occasions where their work has been publicly discussed. Finally, patronage by state funding bodies — so important for the contemporary artist — very often rests upon such public discussion. Once a funding grant is secured, this also becomes an indicator of interest.

So valorisation is something which occurs at a particular point in the cycle of Art production, distribution and consumption, as well as being a continuous process. Entry into the market via the agents of distribution is the point where the Art work finally assumes its full commodity status, but the process of valorisation is also something that must be continuous if the exchange value of the work is to be maintained and increased.

Consumption and reproduction

We have now reached the final stage in the journey taken by the work of Art in its transformation into a cultural commodity; *the moment of consumption.* If you visit an exhibition, you will notice that certain works have a small red dot attached to their mounts or frames. This indicates that the work has been sold. If you look around the gallery — and often you have to search quite hard — you will be able to obtain the list of prices that are being asked for the works. My guess is that although there will be some degree of price variation, the works will lie within a fairly narrow range. Where there is a significant discrepancy this is largely due to the degree of interest that has already clustered around the work of that particular artist. So who is buying?

This will very much depend upon the nature of the show you are visiting. If the prices are not too high then it is likely to be other artists, critics, or modest collectors. Very often major new works by established artists will already be spoken for either by major collectors or by public museums. Any works that remain unsold after the show has finished can be viewed privately since they will be housed in the storage space attached to the gallery. From this point on the works disperse themselves in various directions: into the houses of private collectors; to institutions such as banks, corporations; or to public museums and galleries. Here they will remain waiting for the encounter with the spectator that will bring them to life, or consignment to a state of perpetual obscurity. But each of them, if they are re-sold, will be subject to the same process. That is, in exchange for a given sum of money they will become the property of their purchaser to do as they will with them. This can even extend to their being destroyed, something which happened in the case of Graham Sutherland's portrait of Winston Churchill.

In completing the first circle in the process of Art commodification we have detailed what might be termed *simple reproduction*. That is the artist produces a work which moves through the various stages outlined above. The key moment is the sale of the work and the realisation of its exchange value. With this completed successfully, a return, in the form of money, is made to the artist (the point of production) to enable a fresh round of production to commence. The career of any particular artist, looked at from the perspective of the commodity, could be represented by numerous such circuits each with varying degrees of success. The question to ask at this point is 'What happens if sales do not eventuate?' A number of possibilities are open to the individual who fails to make a sale. The artist may introduce a regime of austerity and continue to survive (and produce) on ever more limited resources. They may be forced to obtain an income by selling their labour in other, non-producing activities. Part-time work or teaching is a much favoured option. They may be lucky and gain some financial support from a state funding institution or foundation, or they may cease artistic production altogether and 'become' something else. The fate of any individual artist is clearly dependent upon the return they are able to secure for their work and this in turn rests upon the rise and fall of the value of artistic labour within the society they live in.

Simple reproduction is not the end of the story of the commodification of Art. It will be noted that a crucial separation takes place in the cycle after valorisation. The work becomes the property of its buyer, while money flows back to the artist. Such a split represents an important feature in the cycle, namely that from this point on the value of artistic labour and the exchange value of the Art commodity are subject to *different* systems of valorisation. For example, works of Art can outlive their makers and yet continue to acquire or lose exchange value, for example, their prices fluctuate. Because works are able to circulate within a system of exchange that is independent from the system which determines the price of artistic labour, this means that their subsequent value is determined in ways other than those we examined at the point of production. How and why these processes of re-circulation and re-valuation (re-valorisation) take place is the subject of the remainder of this chapter.

The re-circulation and re-valorisation of Art

The processes involved in the second phase of Art commodification are very closely tied to the systems of Art marketing that have emerged in the West in the second half of this century. There have always been Art economies — in the sense of their being mechanisms for distributing the products to the place, persons and situations for which they are required — though not necessarily in the form of the contemporary Art market. There have always been mechanisms of *simple reproduction* whereby the makers with the necessary skills are ensured a return — monetary or otherwise — to enable production to continue. The exceptions to this are those occasions where a society undergoes a complete collapse either for reasons of internal disintegration or because of conquest by external force. However this assertion has always to be seen from the general point of view. Individual producers may 'go to the wall', but from the perspective of a society as a whole, the conditions for Art production are reproduced.

What marks the current situation off as different has been the rise and eventual domination of an *investment market* in Art objects. Art objects have become a favoured area whereby wealth is deployed (invested) in order to both preserve the value of that wealth and, if possible, make it create more wealth. In such a system it is the exchange value of the Art objects which dominates over their use value. For instance, the use value of an Art work can be utterly suppressed by placing the work in a bank vault, but the exchange value of this vaulted object may increase none the less. This increase in the importance of the exchange value of Art can lead to situations where Art works are worth astronomical sums of money, but where contemporary conditions for the production of new Art can be very unfavourable. Art objects, in this type of market, continue to be traded and each time such a transaction takes place the exchange value of the works may rise or fall. This means that we can now locate a second point of valorisation and what has already been said about this process in the cycle of simple reproduction applies here even more forcibly.

Investments in Art

On the surface the rise of an investment market in Art may appear to be relatively straightforward. Investment simply refers to the fact that there has been a generalised movement of wealth into the purchasing of Art works as a way of ensuring the maintenance and increase of the value of that wealth. Why such a move has occurred is to do with the general transformations that have taken place in the economies of the Western nations since World War II. *How* such Art investment takes place is more complex and ultimately rests upon a number of interlocking factors to be detailed below.

That such investments in Art occur is, by now, common knowledge. What is perhaps less well known is the degree of precision with which it is monitored, the enormous amounts of wealth that are at stake and the degree to which it closely resembles analogous markets in stocks and shares. The reason for this unfamiliarity is perhaps owing to the fact that Art as investment is more likely to surface in the financial pages of newspapers and journals than in the more obviously Art-orientated publications. It is common to encounter in such pages 'League Tables' for Art — here the rise and fall in the prices of the work of particular artists, movements or periods, are laid out in the form of a graph to enable the reader/investor to judge where the best investment may be made (*see* Fig. 5.1).

The first feature of the contemporary art market that needs stressing is its international character. One might imagine it as rather like a pyramid with the topmost layer consisting of a number of *auction houses* which have become recognised as the main conduits through which expensive Art must pass if it is to command prices large enough to increase a work's exchange value. The names of such auction houses are famous — *Sotheby's* and *Christie's* being the most well known. They are organised along the lines of multi-national corporations with offices located in each of the major Art dealing cities. (London and New York are the acknowledged centres for such trade.) Below this level there are complex networks operating at the national and regional levels which exist to channel Art objects to prospective purchasers. When an important work or collection comes onto the market the auction will be organised in one of the major Art trading cities, but always with a complex electronic network in place to enable bidders to participate worldwide, and it is common these days for a work valued in millions of dollars to be purchased over the

Sotheby's Art Index
SEASONAL PRICE CHANGES BY SECTOR

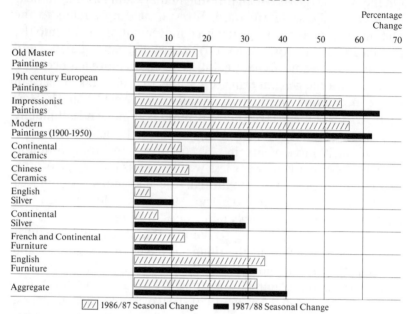

	1986/87 Seasonal Change	1987/88 Seasonal Change

Reproduced, courtesy of Sotherby's

Figure 5.1

telephone. In this sense Art, like stocks and shares or commodities futures, is one of a number of resting places for the ceaseless flow of money on the international capital market. Once this Art trading system is in place then it is no different from any other financial market. Once it is seen that investment in Art is capable of producing the required return for a given outlay of capital, then the more investing institutions will be drawn towards it and the more the exchange value of the works will rise. Increasingly the purchasers of major works of Art are not museums or galleries, but investment houses or multi-national corporations that have assigned a portion of their vast funds for Art investment. In the UK the pension fund of one of the major rail unions entered the Art market as a way of diversifying their assets and they now have a respectable Art collection which is open to the public. The giant UK advertising firm of Saatchi and Saatchi have a huge collection of contemporary Art which is housed in their own gallery in London. The entry of just one large buyer into the field of Art investment can disrupt even the state-funded institutions' ability to purchase the Art of their own country. This is exactly what happened when the Getty Foundation began purchasing. This foundation was established out of the huge fortune amassed by the oil industrialist J. P. Getty. So great are its funds that its purchasing ability appears able to outstrip all but the most wealthy corporations. Certainly no state-funded institution is able to compete with it and many of these institutions have to rely upon the restrictions which many countries place upon the export of Art works in order to remain in the game. This topmost layer of the Art market may appear to be rather remote from the more modest dealings in Art that most of us are familiar with. But there are fall-outs from this high finance which affect the lower levels of the Art market pyramid. There is a discernible 'knock-on' effect whereby inability to compete at the topmost level entails a shift of funds and of interest to other areas. Relatively minor works by major artists, as well as minor works by minor artists become objects of interest and therefore experience an increase in their exchange value. What then starts to happen is a two-fold process — as individuals learn that Art objects are a viable form of investment, increasing numbers of people start to do just that — invest! As the number of investors increases and the amount of money invested rises an ever-widening circle of objects is drawn into the process of investment commodification. Uninteresting forms of Art, semi-industrial artifacts, and obscure regional forms all begin to acquire a nimbus of charm, a sure sign that they are becoming objects of valorisation. Once again, it needs to be stressed that this does not necessarily imply an ever-widening circle of opportunity for young artists. Art investment, like any other form of investment rests upon a calculable degree of risk and therefore a calculable degree of safety. By and large the work of young contemporary artists rarely satisfies the arithmetic of the company accountant.

Scarcity

Given the presence of this structure of Art investment then certain other subsidiary mechanisms can be identified that impinge upon and influence the overall exchange value of a work.

The most obvious of these is scarcity. The simple law of supply and demand would indicate that the fewer the number of desired objects for sale and the greater the number of potential buyers, then the higher the price. The creation of scarcity can take a number of forms in the Art market. If a well-known artist produced only relatively few works, then the purchase of one of those works would usually entail more money than would those of an artist who was prolific. It is still possible to purchase a small print by Picasso for a relatively small outlay, whilst anything by Seurat is likely to fetch a very high price. An artist's work may be scarce because the bulk of their output is in the hands of public institutions. Such institutions tend not to sell their works — or only infrequently, which means that the number of major works by major artists in private hands is constantly decreasing and therefore the number appearing on the open market is less and less. Today it is virtually impossible for an institution with limited funds to put together a representative collection of French Impressionist or post-Impressionist works. Being highly prized, they tend to be kept despite their enormous value. Nowadays, the few examples that do come up for sale will be way beyond the purchasing power of many museums and galleries. They are lucky if they can afford to purchase Kandinsky's socks! Dealers and auction houses have been known to intervene in order to artificially maintain the scarcity of an artist's work and so keep up prices. We saw earlier that many dealers have exclusive contracts with artists who agree to sign over all the work they produce over a number of years. Should the artist die then such contracts may even apply to all unsold works. If all the work of an artist were released onto the market at the same time the subsequent glut would very likely depress the prices. By careful rationing of the remaining work their exchange value is maintained.

Changes of taste

The economic value of a work, or a particular category of works, can be significantly altered by the inevitable changes in taste that take place over any period of time. Such shifts in taste affect the exchange value of art works. The example of British Victorian painting will illustrate what I mean.

In the 19th century certain painters were not only very famous, but were rich as well and a good proportion of their wealth came from the record prices that their works were fetching at the time. Such artists *Sir* John Millais, *Sir* Lawrence Alma-Tadema, *Lord* Frederick Leighton and *Sir* Edward Poynter were able to sell their works for enormous sums. The arrival and eventual dominance of European artistic Modernism in the UK (just before World War I, but especially in the 1920s) — led to a re-evaluation of Victorian

Art. It fell out of favour, being seen as academic, stilted, sentimental and literary. There was a general depression of the works of the period both culturally and economically. This anti-Victorian taste was part of a much wider criticism of Victorian beliefs and social habits that the first generation of British post-Victorians mounted as the United Kingdom finally moved into the 20th century. Thus much of the Art which previously had been both popular and expensive was now to be had for prices *less than* those paid when the works were first sold. We can trace the fortunes of one of these paintings from the sales records.

The Finding of Moses by Sir Lawrence Alma-Tadema was sold in 1904 for £5,250 (this is on top of the fact that the person who commissioned the work paid all of the artist's expenses for a long stay in Egypt researching the picture.)

Figure *Date of Sale*	*Price in £* *Sterling*
1904	5,250
1935	861
1942	273.10s.
1960	252

Figure 5.2

By the middle of the 1960s the long rejection of the Victorians and their Art began to change. In the late 1960s a work by Sir Lawrence Alma-Tadema was sold for the same price that was originally paid for it and ever since then prices for Victorian Art have risen steeply. In 1986 a work by Sir Edward J. Poynter (a contemporary of Alma-Tadema) was sold for about $450,000. This is not because Victorian taste and sensibility has returned, rather that Victorian painting has been re-interpreted and re-valorised. It would, I think be rather too neat an explanation to claim that the re-interpretation of Victorian Art that has got underway since the mid-1960s was directly caused by the changes in the Art market. A full explanation of this shift in taste would have to look at the forms of anti-Modernism that were beginning to surface within the intellectual elites of the UK. Nevertheless, I would claim that a component of this re-evaluation was the current saturation of the market for Modernist Art. Periods which were previously in disfavour had to be opened up and provided with an 'interest factor' so as to reassure those individuals on the look out for suitable objects to invest in.

Generally one could say that as more money has been directed into Art investment the more objects of past periods acquire both cultural significance and economic value. We have now reached a point where anything more that twenty years old is liable to become an object to be collected. The motto to be learnt from all this is 'Don't throw anything away!'

Valorisation: second phase

The implicit assumption beneath the discussion of the second phase of commodification has been that it almost always applies to works of dead artists or at least to works that have been in circulation for sometime. It is now time to foreground this assumption and examine it more closely.

I have already mentioned that *re-interpretations* of the past are also closely allied with *re-evaluations* of the past. *Taste* is in fact these two operations compressed into a single disposition towards the Art of a particular epoch. We might phrase this slightly differently and say that the process of re-evaluation and re-interpretation involves the replacing of one meaning for a work by another. (This can be either positive or negative). In the case of Victorian Art we saw how the earlier, Modernist inspired interpretation that it was sentimental and stilted was replaced by a 1960s view that it interpreted as whimsical, nostalgic, and surreal. We need to ask the question 'who is responsible for this new interpretation?' Once again we encounter the complex systems of re-valorisation whose effects eventually impinge on the market, creating oscillations in economic value.

Taste makers and Taste making

It is a truism that every age sets about to create a past for itself, but how *that* past is created and *what* an age selects in a particular past for approval and disapproval can never be determined beforehand. Given these qualifications it is possible to identify a set of mechanisms through which such re-evaluations occur and then broaden out to effect the economic value of Art works.

The initial moves in re-interpretations of the past may often be detected within the *intellectual elites* of a society, particularly amongst those personnel charged with the writing of histories. The emergence of new evidence about an epoch, the rise of new intellectual problems, together with the shifts in artistic and philosophical taste brought about by a changed set of cultural conditions, can all contribute in focusing the attention of Art Historians upon previously ignored periods or artists. For instance it wasn't until the onset of Romanticism in the late 18th and early 19th century that Rembrandt was re-interpreted as a great master. Publication of monographs or articles in scholarly journals, even when produced under the neutrality of scholarship cannot but help in drawing the interest of a wider circle of individuals. Within the ranks of the intelligentsia are often to be found eccentric individuals who refuse to conform to the canons of current taste; instead they may champion a set of alternative values and meanings, raising up where others are happily putting down. Such a cultural critic was Sir John Betjeman — a figure who spent his life praising Victorian Art and Architecture when it was most unfashionable. By the 1960s his solitary vigil started to come to an end as intellectuals increasingly began to share his approval for the works of the 19th century.

Such divergencies of taste are common within a society's cultural elites, but it is when they begin to be taken up by the broad spectrum of *cultural mediators* that their effects can be most clearly seen. This group consists of Art reviewers, dealers and gallery owners, curators of Art exhibitions, and the collectors of Art. Once a new interpretation of the past is accepted and gains a foothold within this strata, intellectual interest can quickly get transformed into economic interest. New meanings are equated to new values.

Critical intervention

The bulk of re-valorisation is to do with the Art of the past but the movement of wealth into Art investment has turned the cultural mediator in the present into a powerful and, at times, controversial figure. Perhaps this is nowhere more emotionally charged than in the role of the critic.

Although there have been very powerful Art critics in the past — for instance John Ruskin in 19th-century England was extraordinarily influential in validating the work of new artists such as Turner and the Pre-Raphaelites — it is in the 20th century, particularly since World War II, that the Art critic has become a powerful agent influencing actual Art production. The Art critic can promote the works of an artist simply by drawing the public's attention to them in writing, but they can effect a set of much deeper influences by placing the work of an artist within a framework of comprehension, that is by elaborating a philosophy and a taste whereby the work can be understood and accepted. Any critic who reaches such a position of prominence, whether they like it or not, produces a 'knock-on' effect upon the Art market. They are read, they are taken notice of and can (either directly or indirectly) influence the flows of wealth into certain areas. The New York critics of the 1950s and 1960s, particularly Clement Greenberg and Harold Rosenberg, were pivotal in validating the work of the Abstract Expressionists. So effective was their powerful interpretation that the works of this school were highly sought after.

For the artist who is the recipient of such critical approval this can be exhilarating and if the work begins to sell then the temptation is either to produce more of the same or maintain market interest by introducing a degree of novelty into the work — but not too much to confuse the collectors. I do not wish to convey the impression that every aspect of an epoch's production can be cynically reduced to an effect of the market, but likewise it would be foolish to ignore the impact that such a battery of eyes has upon how an artist operates.

The artist as personality

Since the onset of Romanticism in western Europe artists have been an object of intrigue, fascination and horror for the non-Art public. One only has to recall the cult of the personality which surrounded the romantic English poet, Lord Byron in the early part of the 19th century. What they are, how they behave has been almost as important as what they produce. Since World War II this personality cult has intensified with certain artists approximating to film stars. This publicity of the personality of the artist has become a crucial element in the creation of interest, with the result that works can become saturated with the meanings that have accreted around the figure of the artist. For example, it is almost impossible to look at Jackson Pollock's late 'drip' paintings without calling up the famous photographs taken in 1950 by Hans Namuth, of the artist at work in his Long Island studio. As Art has become both an area of investment *and* a spectator sport, so the publicity surrounding artists and their private activities has increased. Two processes are operating within this type of Art publicity — the straightforward valorisation of an artist who is *selected* for such attention. The message here is 'this artist is worthy of *your* interest'. But, publicity can go further as it attempts to construct a distinctive personality out of which the works are thought to have emerged. This linking of the work to the personality of the artist is seen to somehow *explain* the work — a hectic and scandalous life = hectic and scandalous work. Perhaps the epitome of this process was Andy Warhol, who literally vanished into the publicity which eventually *became* him. The work became a sign of 'Warholness' and some would say that the publicity was far more interesting than anything the man himself produced. To own a work by a highly publicised artist becomes a way of owning a piece of that life; the more vivid the life, the more desirable the Art.

Movement labelling

One of the most prominent features of 19th-century and 20th-century Art, or at least one of the features of the standard story of the Art of modern times, is the prevalence of artistic movements, or 'isms'. Certainly up until the emergence of Abstract Expressionism, or perhaps even Pop Art, it was possible to see Modern Art as consisting of a succession of 'isms'. Commencing with Realism in the 19th century, each movement gave way to its successor with the 'next thing' going beyond, reacting against, or further developing what its predecessor had laid down. Such an account of artistic change is a very useful narrative for an Art market hungry for new and continuing sources of investment. As one movement appears to exhaust itself the market is able to maintain its buoyancy through the prospect of a new school emerging on the horizon.

This tendency to label movements and place them in a *developmental logic* has two aspects. In the first strategy it is possible to make a reasonably clear distinction between the events which are/or were taking place in Art and the construction of a story which attempts to divide up and label these events into movements. Disputes then rage as to whether such labelled categories ever existed, or there may be attempts to move the labels around, or juggle with the sequences in which they are supposed to have happened. It is *the story*, not necessarily the events, which has the potentiality to collude with the dynamics of the Art market. However, the stories which are constructed about Art are not simply passive reflectors of the real situation 'out there'. They can attain the status of powerful myths and become active shapers of production itself. The desire for the story to continue then becomes an agenda for action. At what point does production begin to conform to and confirm the story which is being told about it? There is more than a suspicion that at about the time that Abstract Expressionism emerged (even I'm doing it) pressures deriving from the market were fuelling a continuation of the 'isms' game. The critic who was first to identify, describe and successfully label a new movement would gain considerable kudos and attention. Dealers or gallery owners who had the new movement as part of their stable of artists were assured of increasing interest in what was for sale, whilst the buyer who was first off the blocks in purchasing these works was guaranteed to acquire both a bargain and something whose exchange value would shortly rise.

What is clear is that after the rise of Abstract Expressionism a plethora of new and often meaningless labels were being affixed to the work of very diverse artists. The pressure upon those writing about the Visual Arts is to detect unity, similarities, and play the game of groupings — spotting the 'new group' is an endemic activity in writing about Art. Reviewers scan works for signs of emerging national schools or schools based upon region or locality. Works get arranged together on the basis of race, class or gender. Revivals of earlier Art styles, or earlier sensibilities may all be utilised to establish common meanings or common frameworks through which the objects can be allotted an immediate place within Art History. A secure place in the story can lead to the objects becoming securities in the economic sense.

The signs of Art

We have now reached the final stage in the discussion of Art as a commodity. I want to bring the discussion to a close by examining some of the repercussions which the production and circulation of Art objects has beyond the traffic in the objects themselves — that is how *the signs of Art* enter into the traffic in images.

One way to accumulate a collection of modern art for minimal cost is to obtain copies of the catalogues which the major auction houses put into circulation before a major sale. Inside such publications one can find quality colour reproductions of many of the works to be sold, together with a detailed description of the work along with its *provenance*. (The provenance of a work of Art is the list of all of its previous owners where known.) Of course, one is only acquiring the work in reproduction, but for the majority of us, reproduction is all that is available. This fact of reproduction, or more accurately repetition, has opened up yet another dimension to the area of Art as commodity. Together with *simple reproduction* and the re-circulation of Art objects, we must now add the circulation and traffic in the reproductions of Art works.

To understand the full complexity of this third stage we have to return to the earlier distinction between use value and exchange value. We have seen that at a certain point in the exchange system the Art work 'unhooks' itself from the labour of the artist and becomes an independent economic entity, a commodity. We also saw that having been transformed into a commodity it is perfectly possible for it to have *no* immediate use value, but still be able to maintain its exchange value. (The work of Art in the bank vault). With the emergence of the technology of reproduction it is now possible for the exchange value to be maintained, but for a whole new set of use values to be generated through the work being reproduced. So pervasive is the phenomenon of reproduction that it is difficult to detail all the ways in which such reproductions are used. A few examples will have to suffice. The clearest instances occur in those areas most closely associated with the functioning of the Art world.

- auction house catalogues that have already been mentioned
- photographic slides used in teaching
- Art Historical books. (All the illustrations you will encounter in this Volume have to be paid for.)
- The sales counters of museums
- Exhibition catalogues

All of these instances represent both *points of reproduction* and *points of sale* where the repetitions, or signs, of the original work of Art are distributed and dispersed and where new use values for the work — or the signs of it — are realised. Just as the production of the original work involved labour so the production of the reproductions also entails labour. To purchase these *reproductions* you must be able to afford the price and, as always, a portion of this money is returned to the makers of the *reproductions* in order to ensure that the conditions of *production* of the *reproductions* are reproduced. With the reproduction of a work there is also a tendency for *interest* to be generated and the more it is encountered in reproduction the more likely its exchange value is to rise. But the effects of reproduction extend further and drive deeper than this.

One of the more famous works of modern European literature is a book by the Austrian writer Robert Musil, entitled *The Man Without Qualities*. He wrote this in the early part of the century

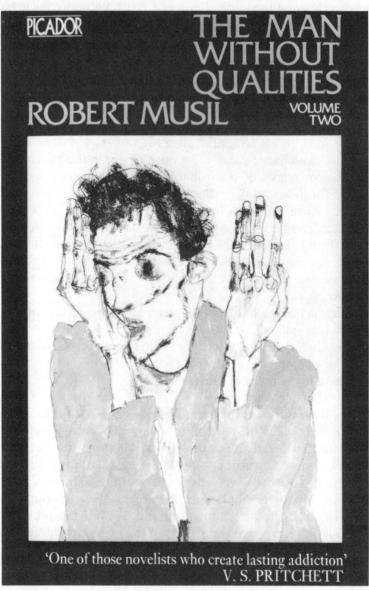

32. Bookcover
(Pan Books Ltd, London)

whilst he was living in Vienna. I have encountered a English paper-back translation of this work and on its cover was a reproduction of a painting by the Viennese artist Egon Schiele (*see* ill. 32).

Schiele was born in 1890 and died in the influenza epidemic which swept Europe in 1918. Musil was born in 1880 and studied in Berlin for a number of years, eventually returning to Vienna in 1914 when World War I began.

I suppose that the novel by Musil and the painting by Schiele were brought together in order that a particular set of associations might be generated in the book browser's mind. Late 19th-century/early 20th-century Vienna is seen as a major contributor to the formation of European Modernism. Not only did Musil and Schiele live there, but other key figures of intellectual and artistic Modernism such as Freud, Schoenberg, the architect Adolf Loos, the artist Gustav Klimt, and the writer Arthur Schnitzler were present too. Over the years a quite particular meaning has been constructed around Vienna at this time; introspection, the alienated self, pain, anxiety, an amiable decadence and difficult Art. The operation taking place with this edition of Musil is that the novel and the painting have been soldered together to produce the connotation of *Vienneseness*. They produce in the browser a feeling that somehow book and image refer naturally to one another, have a complementary relationship and of course share something in common. The sign of the original Art work — the reproduction — has been put to a new use value. The point I wish to stress here is that as the link between the original Art work and its reproduction gets weaker and weaker (very often only a detail of the original will be utilised) the original may eventually evaporate altogether. In the case of the book cover a knowledge of Modern Art History may ensure that the reader knew that it was a reproduction of a Schiele painting (usually there is a citation placed on the back cover) but someone lacking such knowledge would not immediately make the connection and would be afloat on a sea of connotated 'Vienneseness'. Again the instances where art works are used to either sell, or impart connotations to other commodities are far too extensive to detail here.[1]

The fact that most of us now tend to encounter a work in reproduction before we encounter the original has the effect of changing the meaning which the original work has for us. The sight of it can be bizarre and perhaps even disappointing. We may experience a shock by realising that it actually, does exist somewhere. But this process can be taken even further. It is possible to discern in certain visual media such as video-clips, record covers, magazine layouts, even contemporary works of Art, 'ghosts' of an earlier 'original'. By this stage the links referring back to the original are extremely tenuous. What remains is the feel of Art in general or a flavour of past periods, tastes and styles. The domain of Art has now become a generalised aesthetic field in which signs echoing to an original are used to fuel fresh rounds of production and consumption.

We can now represent the various stages in this complex process by way of the following diagram.

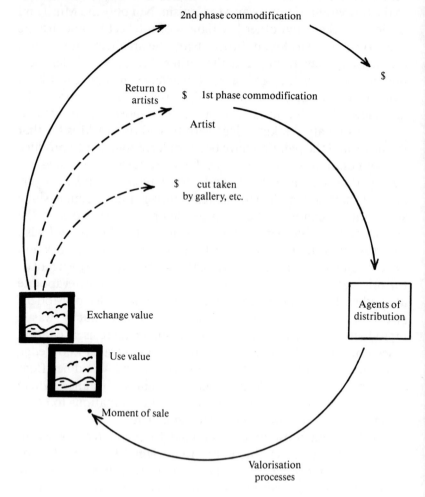

Figure 5.3

By the time a few laps around the Art commodification circuit have been completed the exchange value of the original can become so concentrated and massive as to be almost radioactive with economic value. The system may begin to undergo some bizarre transformations where the only use value possible for the work is its astronomical exchange value. It is this economic value which *is* the work so that one owns not an image X by the artist Y, but something which is worth Z millions − the work, quite literally, has become treasure.

For the *Sunflowers* (by Van Gogh) have worked. Everyone was puzzled that a Japanese company could pay so much for a work of art, but Yasuda's art gallery used to be more or less deserted. Yasuda bought a couple of Renoirs and attendance rose a bit. Then came the *Sunflowers*. Now the visitors stand in a queue to catch the life to the 42nd floor.

The gallery − and, of course, the company − is on the map.[2]

1   The classic examination of the continuities between the tradition of Western painting and the language of modern advertising is to be found in John Berger *Ways of Seeing* Harmondsworth: Penguin, 1972, esp. chapter 7, pp. 129-54.
2   Hamish McRae 'Japan's sunflower solution' *Guardian* (London) 30 October 1987.

6
From object to text

We have already begun to register some of the ways in which the Art object — as an ensemble of symbolic forms and signs — has a double aspect. It comes out of, and bears the traces of, the complex processes that were at work in the moment of production. But it is also an object which by its very nature is already turning its face towards its potential spectator. However much we might attempt to explain its complex construction through a consideration of the elements involved in this production, it is something which always emerges from this birth primed and ready for its encounter with this viewer. Again we only need to recall the earlier remarks about coding in general where it was stated that to operate successfully a minimum of *two* positions were required — a *sender* and a *receiver*. In fact we might define an image as 'something which is made to be looked at by someone, from somewhere, in some way(s)'. Chapters 7, 8, and 9 will discuss the elements of *someone, somewhere* and *someway(s)*.[1]

But, as we found in the section on production, the systematic probing of the boxes in the model always involved a consideration of the arrows which linked adjacent elements. We found the boxes were, in reality, a series of relationships and not things that could be regarded as isolated and discrete entities. Much of what is referred to as 'the new theory' began with the ways in which spectator and object interact with one another. How and why this theoretical shift has occurred will be one of the recurrent subsidiary themes of this section. For the moment, it is perhaps sufficient to remark that this move was undertaken to overcome a gap within what we might loosely term 'Modern Art' and the theory which accompanied it. What was missing within Modernism was a fully formulated set of ideas about precisely what role the spectator played within the aesthetic circuit. (This was certainly not the case in the ideas about Art which circulated in the West before the arrival of Romanticism.) Repeatedly one can see Modernist theories about Art explaining the effectivity of the Art object by either emphasising the act of production — the activity of making became the site where the essence of the work resided. Or, they inserted the spectator into Box I; the success of the work was then gauged according to the degree to which the ideas or emotions which the maker had towards their work were reproduced *within* the spectator. In both cases Box II (the object) became the terminal point of the discussion, with the works being accorded an extraordinary power in and of themselves. They were seen either as the harbingers of a new and brighter world, or simply as traces left behind by the intensity experienced by artists as they engaged in the processes of making.

I want to open up this discussion of the place of the viewer by looking at the nature of this 'turning-towards-the-spectator' within the Art object. This represents, perhaps, the most significant theoretical shift in recent years and is marked in the literature by a terminological change. We might summarise this by saying that there has been a move from regarding the Art work as *an object*, to regarding it as *a text*.

What does this change in terminology — the substitution of the term 'text' for 'object' — signify? On the surface it may seem that all we are dealing with is a slight shift of emphasis — from maker to viewer. Certainly, this is part of the move. But behind this apparently minor adjustment lies a revolution in the ways the Visual Arts are being thought about and the ways in which they are being made. Many have even likened it to a move as profound as that which occurred in the shift from Newtonian physics to that of Einstein. We might say it placed the weight of our investigations upon the arrows that link the boxes in the model with the Visual Arts increasingly formulated in terms of *a set of shifting relationships* rather than a collection of discrete atoms, where the boxes approximate to the actions and re-actions of colliding billiard balls.

For most of what we term the 'Modern period', the location of the Art object within the domain of production was seen as constituting *the* explanation of Art. Seeing the Art work either in terms of its emergence out of the processes of production, or as an outcropping from within the artist has had enormous significance within Art History. The best way to grasp this is to reformulate our founding model into a linear causal sequence:

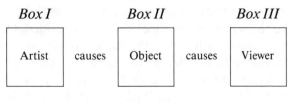

Figure 6.1

In fact this is really a formulation in which the explanation for the object and the viewer ultimately reside within Box I. This means that so long as we are able to have access to enough information concerning Box I − either about the artist as an individual, or of the factors impinging upon the process of production − then the rest of the diagram should fall into place. Of course, such a model can also approximate to a theory of *historical sequence and causation*, with each successive box being simply an effect caused by the previous stage. The ultimate origins of everything, that is its founding moment, are seen as residing within the artist or within the elements of production.

This linear model has become sedimented into the very foundations of Art History and claims to have explained the Art object when it has determined each stage by a set of antecedent causes whose base line is the 'artists themselves'. It also has the force of commonsense to back it up. 'Surely it is obvious that it is the artist who is responsible for creating the work?' The terminology for such a model is *productivist* and *historicist*. It is a type of explanation which locates the source of artistic and cultural phenomena within the realms of production and by conceiving the Art work as the outcome of an antecedent series of historical causes.

The first thing to grasp about the term 'text' is that it is not containable within the outlines of Box II in the same way that the term 'object' is. It must be thought of as always carrying an arrow linking it to Box III, the place of the spectator. In other words the term text always indicates a-turning-towards.

This choice of words is important because it signals that a text is not an *object*, a physical thing, but *a process*. It carries within it the implication that a text is to be seen, to be looked at, to be grasped by a viewer. Put another way, a text is the process of reaching out towards, or an invitation to come in. It is not a physical quality of the object but a characteristic which derives from already being embedded in a relationship to an implied viewer. So a text is *that* relationship, or at least one element of that relationship, since, in the realm of textuality it always takes at least two to tango.

What are the implications which flow from this formulation of the text? I would suggest that, in terms of our diagram they are two fold. Firstly it up-ends the simple linearity of Figure 6.1 (p. 126) and transforms it into a circuit. Secondly it always transforms the single arrow into a pair.

The object is the physical thing that was made by someone, in some place, at some time. For instance:

Artist: Velasquez
Title: Las Meniñas
Date: 1656
Place: The Prado Museum, Madrid
Dimensions: Height 3.18m/width 2.76m
Medium: Oil paint

The text is that which is encountered by someone else, in another place, at another time. The theoretical formulation 'the object' suggests a physical thing that can be located by its artist, time and place. The text is all the subsequent meanings which are generated in all of its subsequent encounters. This means that the text is a *continuing process* of meaning production.

We are now in a better position to see how the idea of an artistic text, rather than an artistic object, radically disturbs the normal methods of practising Art History. It might be said that Art History considered that it had done its job − that is produced an explanation − if it managed to explain the Art work in terms of a result of a set of historical antecedents. The object/Art work was seen as primarily, something that was located in the past, 'back there'. Its task was to carefully refine and improve upon all previous historical explanations. The idea of text carries within it the idea of a continuous and changing set of encounters up until the

33. Velasquez: *Las Meniñas* 1656 (The Prado Museum, Madrid)

present, none of which are to be accorded a priority over the others. It is important to realise that the physical object may remain the same, while the text only emerges within each encounter. So our *Las Meniñas* is not the same *Las Meniñas* that Velasquez painted in 1656. Each encounter with the text of *Las Meniñas* is a potential re-production of it. It is important to remember that *text* is concerned with the dimensions of meaning and the theoretical change that is taking place largely rests upon advances made in the investigation of meaningfulness.

I've chosen illustration 34, not for its qualities as good or bad

Art, but because of the recurrent benign irritation that it has continued to cause me since I first encountered it over twenty-five years ago. It is possible to approach this Victorian image with the aim of trying to determine what it *meant* when it first appeared. This I could do by listing its various elements — the geology of the cliffs, the sunset, the comet in the sky, the beach, and other features. We might then move on to establish what each of these components meant both to the artist and to the Victorian Art public it was aimed at. The image is then established as an entity with a set of knowable historical elements and explanation becomes a relatively simple computation of the meanings that existed within the period of its production. Such a simple historicist approach may be eschewed in favour of a deeper interpretation. Here there is the assumption that the true meaning of the work can only be grasped by moving below the surface of these elements. That is the true meaning resembles a kind of secret which it is the task of the analyst to reveal or uncover. This 'deeper' reading may frame the picture as embodying a complex set of anxieties lodged at the heart of English middle class optimism in the 19th century. Could it possibly be a visual analogue to a poem written by Matthew Arnold entitled 'Dover Beach' which begins

34. William Dyce: *Pegwell Bay, Kent — a recollection of October 5th 1858.* 1859-60. Oil on canvas, 635mm x 889mm (Tate Gallery, London)

The Sea of Faith
Was once, too, at the full, and round earth's shore
Lay like the folds of a bright girdle furled.
But now I only hear
Its melancholy, long, withdrawing roar,
Retreating, to the breath
Of the night-wind, down the vast edges drear
and naked shingles of the world.

Both the retreating sea and the exposed cliffs may then be seen as a way of visually embodying that complex interplay within Victorian society of the ambiguities surrounding religious faith and the hammering it had received at the hands of geologists such as Lyell and Darwin who were undermining the biblical accounts of the history of the world. We might even incorporate psychoanalytic elements and note the absence of the ubiquitous paterfamilias amongst the group. God and the father going the same way as the tide and the setting sun.

As Dyce painted this picture in 1859-60 and Matthew Arnold published his poem in 1867, this would seem to rule out Dover Beach as a 'source' for the painting and cast doubts upon the truth value of the explanations advanced above. However, if we re-cast this image as text, then it is possible to move away from trying to seek the 'truth' of the image and instead focus on it as a perpetual process of becoming meaningful. I can glance up from my writing and look at a reproduction of this painting that I have stuck above my desk. When I look at it I am not transported back to 1858 (the date of the scene depicted), I encounter it in my here and now. I can see it *through* the Arnold poem. That becomes an element of my reading. Beyond that all I really know is that it is the placing of the figures in relation to one another; the particular pattern of spacings between them. Again and again I am drawn to examine the ways in which they turn away from one another. I am always caught by the look of the women on the right who looks out of the picture towards *me*. But this never reaches the level of *a* meaning. It is never finally fixed. Each time I look into it, it is nothing which emerges out of the image. All I can do is catch myself within an unutterable sadness. It doesn't *mean* sadness, it *is* sadness.

Of course, it could be argued that all we are describing is a process whereby an object which once had a set of determinable meanings, undergoes, with the passage of time, dispersal and fragmentation. But this is to beg the question which it was our aim to dislodge, namely that becoming a text is something that always happens after production has taken place. The full implications of the move from object to text will only become clear if it is realised that we have been dealing with texts all along. It is here that the notion of a text begins to disturb all the other elements of the model. Again commonsense would seem to confirm the idea that it is the artist who is the producer of the meanings which are deposited in the Art object. However, it should be noted in Figure 6.2 that we encounter a double set of arrows. We must now examine more fully the implications of that second arrow between boxes II and I.

Figure 6.2

We have all grown up with the idea that Art works are special precisely because of the unity which they display, and this unity is seen as deriving from either the particular qualities of their maker or from their embodying a set of constructive principles raised to a high level of intensity. In short we like to see them as 'wholes' forming a seamless pattern, sometimes of extraordinary complexity. Put another way the image might be likened to a single harmonious chord and we marvel at the harmonics of the object. To pursue the musical metaphor for a while, we might say that text invites us to move from the harmonics of a single chord over to something more akin to a collection of chords, multiple melodies, sounds and language. The closest I can get to this is to say that text approximates to rapidly turning the dial on a radio. The point is that the lower arrow in Figure 6.2 moves into the very processes of production; production becomes the assembly area where codes, visual conventions, half-formed memories, dismembered remnants of previous images all collide. So a text emerges out of other texts. One might say that text is a theory of permanent loose ends. The passage of time is not a passage from unity to fragmentation, but from variety and difference to variety and difference.

We must now attempt to examine what is perhaps one of the most contentious assertions of the new theory, something that gets indicated by the catchphrase 'the death of the author'. By placing a reverse arrow between the domains of production and object a certain degree of scattering ensues at the level of the works symbolic unity. But as maybe gathered from the phrase 'the death of the author' it is the figure of the artist that is the target of this assault.

Earlier I made the observation that Modernist theories of Art had generally either ignored the position of the spectator or had subsumed it within the role of the maker of the objects, the artist. This is backed up by an enormous body of work which has concentrated upon artists. Who they are, what they are and how they do it? The great difficulty in tackling this area is that there have been, and still are a great many submerged myths, wishes and anxieties at work in and around the common stereotype of 'the artist'. To make matters worse power, careers and money are heavily invested in maintaining a whole battery of fictions in and around the figure of the artist. (To a lesser degree a similar, if less substantial set of investments are at play on the opposite side.)

The phrase 'the death of the author' is not simply something applicable to the literary Arts — authors in a literal sense — but is intended to encompass all those theories which see the singular artist as the originator of a work. So 'author' in this wider sense means the imaginary construct from whom the work is thought to flow. But it is more than this, because the term author refers to how we comprehend the work. When we look at a work by Kandinsky it is thought that we are also in some way encountering the author Kandinsky. So author is meant to identify that very complicated set of assumptions about Art whereby we imagine the meaning of an image to be located either in the psychology/personality of the artist, or within the *life* of the artist. (We can also reverse the terms of these equations, it makes no difference to the status of the term 'author'.) The personality or life of the artist lies to one side and the object to the other and between the two terms are a battery of linking concepts which aim to join the two entities together in a particular way. Such a word is 'expression' in the sentence 'The artists express themselves in the works'. Or 'reflection' in 'the image reflects the life of the artist', or 'intention' in 'the artist meant x, y and z when he/she painted this picture'. Whatever the terminology, the aim is similar in that the Art object becomes an effect of, is 'authored' by a particular entity 'the artist'. We encounter the manifestations of authorship in other ways too, for instance in the copyright laws and in the artist's signature placed in the corner of the work. As one critic has observed when taken as a whole the relation between an author and their works starts to resemble that of a father to his progeny. They bear his name and are in some sense, part of him. The anti-author arguments are drawing attention to the fact that authors do not have *total control* over the nature of the work they produce (their oeuvre). We seem able to accommodate this 'lack of control' quite comfortably when we talk about the work of Art as an economic value, we have many more difficulties in accepting its validity when we look at the work from the angle of the production of its meanings.

This much is clear. But, beyond such certainties, there lie the far murkier realms of anxiety and fantasy which concern themselves with what might be described as an irrational desire to maintain (or establish) the rights of paternity. During the 19th century the artist and their activities became the focus of a great deal of compensatory activity, both by the non-artistic public and artists themselves. As work in general became increasingly routinised, bureaucratised, standardised, and abstracted, artists were constructed as the sorts of people who in their activities and their products were able to resist such tendencies. They were seen, and thought of themselves, as individuals who maintained an intense form of non-alienated work where self, activity and product were held in an intimate and intense relationship. So familiar is this linkage between Art work and author that it is difficult for us to think of any other sorts of relationship. At its centre is a moral desire in which great Art is produced by great artists who are great people.

Against this it is possible to detect a counter-image which also has its own baggage of myths and anxieties, but which has an equal claim to be looked at seriously. There is an increasing suspicion that the forms of exaggerated individualism that have accompanied theories about artistic production may be a little overdone. This has been accompanied by a desire to throw light upon the social and collective processes that may be at work in art. Many artists in the 20th century have been critical of individualistic notions of authorship and this has been particularly the case where these artists were keen to identify themselves and their work with socialistic political movements. In addition to this there is the evidence provided by the new Arts — particularly cinema — where collective production is the norm. Consideration of how a film is made has led to a revision of our ideas of artistic production in the more individualistic Arts. Finally the rise to dominance of mass forms of culture, particularly those instances where the least important aspect of their appearance is the *individual names* of their producers, have underpinned a far more general move away from seeing the author-artist as the sole source of the work. (Think of your favourite soap opera or pop song. How many of you can name any of its producers or writers?)

What has emerged from this debate? Are there any firm positions that might be put forward?

Firstly the 'anti-authors' are not saying that artists don't make works of Art. They have, they do, and they will continue to make them. The point of the anti-author position is a plea not to collapse *making* into a total process, something that can account for every dimension of the Art work. What they are saying is that we cannot transfer the physical generation of an Art object onto the symbolic level. Authors may make the object but they do not *make* the symbolic systems that the text rests in in the same way. Again the example of language is useful here. I am clearly 'responsible' for writing this book, but I have not authored the English language in writing it.

We have already seen that in both the areas of physical production and coding the artist enters into a whole series of social relations which cannot be explained in terms of authorship. There are enormous areas of non-conscious, but structured rules of operation such that it is nonsense to talk as if the work bubbled up from within the artist by magic or sheer will power (even though it may feel like this).

We have also seen that even if ideas about artistic authorship were correct, we still have to confront the question of the encounter between the work and the spectator. This dimension cannot and should not be held within the confines of what the author intended, even if it were possible to determine what those intentions were. Criticisms of authorial theories are part of a more general move to look at how and where texts appear rather than what Art objects were.

Finally it has became clear that the tenacity of the theory of artistic authorship has hidden as much as it has revealed. It has stopped us from seeing that there has always been an enormous variety in the types of relationship that may exist between an artist and the work. Artist A may not 'possess' their work in the same way as artist B. Historical circumstances can vary enormously and so therefore can ideas of artistic authorship.

Just as some critics have formulated the catchphrase 'the death of the author' as a way of encapsulating the theoretical moves of recent years, one might also say that we are witnessing 'the death of the object'. I must, of course, immediately qualify this assertion by stating that what is disappearing is the *theoretical construction* of the Art work as object, but its simultaneous *re-appearance* in the form of the theoretical construction *the text*. In other words, the place previously occupied by the term 'object' is being re-configured as the place of the text. I can perhaps best illustrate this by returning to the painting *Pegwell Bay* by William Dyce. In my earlier interpretation of this image I floated the fiction that the painting might possibly have been influenced by the poem *Dover Beach*. This type of explanation is common in Art History where *sources* and influences are sought by the historian in order to construct a set of antecendent (historical) causes for the image in question. However, because of the discrepancies between the dates of the painting and the poem, 'Dover Beach' had to be ruled out as a possible source. In discussing my reading of the painting from my here and now I suggested that excluding the poem as a factor in my understanding of the painting was both unnecessary and impossible. Of course, it (the poem) can no longer be regarded as a source for the painting but it is permissible to utilise it in a reading being conducted from the present. The term *text* points to the fact that all images can be − and usually are − seen in terms of what happens after their initial production. Rather than seeing them as a final point of *intersecting causes* they can be seen as *moments of intertextuality*. That is a reader of them as text will bring to the work their knowledge of other images − those that were produced both before and after a particular work. Every image is inserted into a field of intertextuality made up of the implicit references, ideas and experiences carried within its multiple readers and mobilised by them when they encounter the work. More radically perhaps, the idea of *intertextuality* implies the idea that there is never a unified set of 'true' meanings to a work because it will always appear within an intertextual field of some kind. *Pegwell Bay* never had a true or original meaning which has subsequently undergone dispersal and fragmentation because when it first appeared it did this as a *text* within the various audiences for Art in Victorian Britain as well as for its artist, William Dyce. The

concept of intertextuality doesn't dispel history in favour of a concentration upon on eternal present, it simply asks us to consider
the domain of history as the place where discontinuous readings
of an image have taken place rather than a place where we can
determine how it truly was.

This completes the observations that I wish to make about the
theoretical shift from object to text. This change of terminology
may appear rather minor, but re-formulations within the realm of
ideas very often resemble the needle in a seismograph. They
tremble in response to very deep perturbations in the world
around. The emergence of the concept of a text has not happened
by chance, it has come about as a way of coming to grips with a set
of radical changes that have taken place in the Visual Arts and
beyond.

My own working circumstances will illustrate what I mean. In
teaching my courses at the University of Sydney I rely heavily upon
our slide collection and the library in which there are books with
thousands of photographs of 2-D and 3-D objects. We also have a
photographic department that is able to record exhibitions for
future reference. For most of the time I do not work from
originals. This is compounded in Australia where there is a dearth
of comprehensive collections of 20th century European and North
American Art. Thus my normal *modus operandi* is with reproductions, not originals.

Text was an idea that was originally formulated in literary
studies where there is no 'original' in the sense that there is in painting and sculpture. For a few dollars we can all own a 'copy' of D. H.
Lawrence's novel *Kangaroo*. As it has become possible to make, on
a large scale, copies/reproductions of Art works, the Visual Arts
have increasingly approximated to the condition of literature. That
is whilst the original may have a specific geographical location, it
is possible for us to have the *text* of a work. We encounter the work
as *text*, not as *object*. I also suspect that for a number of years now
this condition of potential replication is not simply something that
takes place after the advent of the work of Art, but is something
present right from the start. That is images are made either to be
reproduced or as if they were already in a state of reproduction. (In
this, of course, they are being carried along by a set of general
tendencies in our culture in and around the mechanics for the
production and dissemination of all types of information.) This

leads to an intensification of the textualisation of a work and a lessening of its object-ness. Texts are increasingly less dependent upon a particular and locatable physical original. They become more indifferent to their physical medium and more capable of appearing within very different situations. Today, it is the original, physical object which surprises us whilst the reproduction becomes our everyday working tool. So a text, in this sense, can be in many places at the same time whilst the spectator can be in many times at the same place, and unlike the object, we don't have to go to the text, it comes to us.

It is now time to deliver the promise that was made at the beginning of this theoretical interlude, namely to examine the third box in terms of looking at the text in *someway, from somewhere, by someone.*

1　This chapter is based upon the essay by Roland Barthes 'From Work to Text' in the anthology *Image — Music — Text* essays selected and translated by Stephen Heath, London: Fontana, 1977, pp. 155-64.

7
Looking and appearing

The examination of the third box may be separated into three general, but overlapping areas.

Theories of the viewing subject.
Theories dealing with the active role played by the circumstances in which the viewing of Art work is conducted.
Theories concerning the social composition of audiences for Art.

Each of these bodies of theory can be roughly approximated to my earlier claim that a work of Art is an entity that is looked at in someway, from somewhere, by someone.

Theories of the viewing subject — someway

The theories of the spectator or viewing subject may be divided into three broad categories, each one differing in terms of the intellectual traditions upon which they are drawing and the particular aspects of this area that they have chosen to focus on. We have:
- the philosophical subject, that is the subject of knowledge
- the psycho-analytical subject based on theories of psychic subjectivity
- the subject of literary studies, usually known as the reader

Because of their differing intellectual pedigrees each theory constructs the space of the viewing subject in rather different ways. They are really three different maps of Box III, but what unites them all is the central question of how and what sorts of sense are made in the encounter between a text and its reader.

The philosophical subject

One of the most fundamental and persistent divisions within the tradition of Western philosophy is that which separates the world into the realms of mind and matter. The grand divisions of mental/material, subject/object and mind/matter run right through this tradition as well as lodging themselves in our ideas, values and everyday behaviours. So pervasive are these separations that some thinkers have argued that Western thought is nothing other than an extended grappling with the consequences which arise out of such a division. If the world is divided into two domains, qualitatively distinct from each other, how are they ever to be brought together? How does mind or consciousness ever apprehend and gain knowledge of matter? How does a subject ever grasp the object of its consciousness? The tradition of materialism within Western philosophy has tended to explain the realm of mind or consciousness as an outcome, or an effect of, the operations of matter. It is thought of as the consequence of material forces. Mind, in such a schema, should not be seen as significantly different from any other material process. A contemporary version of this is something like molecular biology where the workings of the mind are simply the effects produced by the chemical processes taking place in the brain. The second strand — the tradition of idealism — argues that mind or consciousness underlies or forms matter. In the latter model *knowledge* of objects is only knowledge of our ideas since it is consciousness which is constituting the objects which we then attempt to explain. Mind is only ever able to gain knowledge of itself however much it may feel that it is explaining the world 'out there'.

This may seem abstract and tangential to the nature of Art but it does have some very important implications for the questions surrounding the nature of the viewer. I have argued that cultural objects, in which I include works of Art, do not sit easily within this simple division of the mental and the material. They appear to be entities which straddle this divide in that they are both material objects with a physical composition, but they are also texts which figure in the processes of the production of ideas, emotions and values with varying degrees of success. If we return to our model, particularly the relations between boxes II and III (the viewer and the text) the double set of arrows, suggest that we are in fact dealing with the two logical options we have outlined above — materialism or idealism. Either the Art work is seen as an autonomous object with its meanings simply being characteristics describable in the same way as its physical features or the object and its meanings are simply something which are constituted by its viewer. According to which arrow one decides to stress, this will determine how one then explains what transpires between the two poles. In the first approach it is the object which contains its meanings within itself and these are mechanically reproduced within the subject via the neutral medium of human perception. We might say that in this type of situation we have a 'full' text which places its meanings into an empty subject. In the latter approach (the idealist) it is the subject which contains the meanings (the subject is full) and the Art object which is empty. The Art work then approximates to an empty screen upon which play the wishes, desires and intentions of the viewer. The logical outcome of this position is one in which — at the level of meaning — there can be no 'objective' meanings to the text and, of course, it would also have to argue that there are as many ways of appreciating the text as there are individual viewers. The problem is that whichever side of the Box II/Box III divide one decides to opt for leads to a position which would eliminate the other.

In order to avoid being trapped by either approach the *discreteness* of the terms subject and object has to be breached in some way. (Remember the point made in Chapt. 6, p. 125 where these arrows were to be thought of as processes and relationships rather than as discrete atoms.) This is why I have used the term *coded text* and *turning*. Central to the way I've been describing coding or the coded text is the idea that it always implies two dimensions — the processes engaged in to produce a coded text and the processes engaged with to decode it. While encoding and decoding are distinct operations they are not processes which the producer and viewer engage in at arms length as it were. It is not a situation in which a viewer manipulates the processes of decoding, rather it is a decoder who in the process of decoding *becomes* a viewer.

The concept of turning is crucial because by becoming coded a text acquires a gregarious face. It is ready and primed for an encounter (a decoding). Likewise when individuals occupy the position of subjects desirous of making sense (knowledge) they are also 'turned' towards the text. So, from the point of view of the object decoding is not simply the mechanical transfer of meanings *into* the subject neither is viewing simply a matter of the psychology of perception. Encoding, text and decoding are social processes *in* which both the text and its subject are generated.

All this may seem clear and obvious, simply an exercise in the type of semantics that so often alienates students from theoretical work. But it is an important advance in that it challenges the idea that we view Art objects through two peepholes placed in the skull. Behind the eyes is another us who is looking out, and behind that another one — as if our psyche's resembled the set of a Russian dolls. It is not that we occasionally peep over the walls of the ego, only to duck back into the safety of 'us', rather that the text and the position of subject/viewer come into being along the interference patterns generated by the encounter. Successful pieces of music, paintings or films all operate by being able to transform the space between consciousness and text. They are able to continually reconstitute us and themselves.

The psycho-analytical subject

In modern societies of a capitalist variety, that is societies where market forces tend to dominate the realm of culture in the form of mass media (and where Art is also increasingly under pressure to be both popular and pay for itself in ways other than by State subsidy), we tend to consume culture via a set of individual choices. In such systems we are not forced to attend particular cultural events instead we consume culture because we receive a 'pay off'. We gain *pleasure* from the experience.

Here is an example.

The film industry requires enormous sums of money in order to be able to produce the complex and sophisticated looking product that modern audiences expect. These sums are so large that each new blockbuster becomes newsworthy as the millions of dollars needed for production escalate yearly. Stop and consider for a moment what the phrase 'the film industry' actually means.

Production
Actors
Writers
Technicians
Administrators
— to name just a few of the personnel.

Distribution	Comment
Cinema chains	Critics
Advertising	Film magazines
Multiple copies of the film	Film analysts and teachers
Video	

The term 'film industry' refers to a vast machine organised to make, distribute and show the product 'film'. In order that personnel in the industry be paid, it is necessary that paying customers be lured into cinemas in order that a return be made so that new films can be produced. Without the money derived from ticket sales (and these days all the ancillary spin-offs), then the whole film industry would stop.

Film analysts recognise that as well as the external hardware — there is an inner machinery (software) located within the encounter between the viewer/customer and the film text. This inner machine produces a desire to go the movies, to be entertained and it is that the industry relies on. To understand this crucial moment within the cinematic industry film theorists have started to look at how it is that we (the audiences) gain pleasure from what we see and therefore continue to return to cinemas and pay out our hard-earned money. From its initial surfacing in film studies, this investigation has broadened and acquired a more general aspect, namely what mechanisms are at work in each Art form to produce pleasure in the spectators/consumers. This investigation of the pleasurable aspects of Art and culture has concentrated upon the unconscious (and more rudimentary) elements that are at work in the processes of looking. This move 'down', as it were, to the deep structures of viewing, has carried with it the imprint of psycho-analysis in that these pleasures are equated with certain types of rudimentary sexual structures.

Put very simply, such approaches have pointed to the fact that in media where sight is a crucial element, there exist collective systems organising the visual relationship that we have with the text. That is, when we look at a film or a painting, we don't simply register its presence in a naive way, rather we occupy a prepared position and the occupation of such a position is the key to the success of the medium. It is there, in that place, that pleasurable effects may be secured. The psycho-analytical strand in such theories claims that once we place ourselves within these viewing structures we engage with and re-activate certain processes which resonate with the experiences we had as children. So when we look at a film we are both seeing a series of events and sights unfold on the screen, but we are also re-experiencing a number of very powerful feelings that had to be traversed in our journey from childhood to maturity. The main point to stress here is that these 'things' are not to be thought of as simply 'in' the film. They are not to be situated simply in the content of the particular film we are witnessing, rather they reside in the general features of the encounter between the spectator and the text. For example — a common effect of a successful film is that we 'lose ourselves' in the action taking place on the screen. We identify with the characters who are 'larger than life'. They may re-activate certain fantansies about our parents, but always within a very structured context. We are seated in the auditorium in the dark — a replication of the dream situation perhaps. We look at the characters but they can't 'get at us', therefore there is a base level of security. The screen upon which the film is projected cuts out a window for us through which we can watch the action but remain ourselves invisible. Maybe such a situation allows for us to play with certain infantile conditions where we can — pleasurably — suspend certain components of our adult psyches whose task it is to maintain us in our adulthood.

I think that these psycho-analytically inspired investigations have pointed in two related directions. Firstly it has suggested that subjective experiences such as pleasure, horror, fear, anguish are generated by texts not just by a mechanical triggering of a set of fixed propensities within us. Rather it has suggested that texts carry a certain range of spectator positions within their very coded texture. By occupying these preferred positions the spectator is moved across a range of differing subjectivities. In a film these may be multiple whilst a painting or a photograph may have just a few such 'preferred' positions.

Secondly, it has suggested some of the dimensions that might be in play which allows a text to secure its particular pleasures in so many different spectators. It is only by considering, not the particulars of content, but the structures of viewing, that we can begin to understand the ability of texts to over-ride differences within viewers and so produce common subjectivities. What such theories are saying is not that we are all alike before the encounter with the text, but that a certain point during this encounter we can become alike. We can become an audience.

Literary studies: the reader

The third area of theories of the subject has been elaborated in the area of literary studies, so the construction of the subject here has been termed the position of *the reader* of a text. These studies have tried to determine how the artistic text registers the presence of a reader in its very structure. Its general point is a simple one, namely that texts, as they are generated through the process of coding, carry within themselves a set of features which together add up to what is termed *the implied reader* or *the model reader*. What this suggests is that the interpretation of a text, a reading of it, is not simply a situation of 'anything goes'. For this to happen there would have to be no positions available for an implied reader. Rather it is saying that there are textual features which guide, direct, hint, or enable particular types of reading to be undertaken by the person who occupies this position of implied reader. In a way it is as if a place is being prepared — in the body of the text — for the potential reader to occupy and encounter that text. It is important to stress here the difference between the implied or model reader and the *actual reader*. Circumstances may provide a plentiful supply of actual readers who are also model readers, but with the passage of time wide disparities may occur between the model readers constructed by the text and its actual readers.

Again, it should be stressed that this implied reader is another aspect of the process of turning we have already described. The text itself carries this place and when it is occupied by a co-operative reader — that is someone willing to play the game according to the rules — a reading takes place which *completes* the processes which are carried in the text. It is at this point that *meanings* are generated.

To reiterate, the notion of the work of Art as a coded text necessarily implies the existence of producers/coders and viewers/decoders. Thus the model reader of a text must be someone who either participates in the code or is at least willing to attempt a decoding. A potential reader/viewer who refuses to enter at this level can never be either an actual reader or an implied one. One of the continuing problems of Modern Art is a widespread refusal to enter the spirit of the game by large numbers of potential readers. We may say that at this basic level every text selects a model of an implied reader by choosing to utilise a specific set of codes.

I can perhaps best illustrate the ways in which texts construct implied readers by detailing a few examples. A text may choose to avail itself of a particular set of stylistic devices which presuppose the existence of a model reader both willing and able to be carried along by such flourishes. We are all familiar with the difficulties that many modern readers have with novels written in the 19th century with their long descriptive passages. Modern actual readers may resort to 'skimming' in order to extract the essence of the action. Actual readers in the 19th century delighted in this exact linguistic characterisation.

A similar difficulty confronts modern actual reader/viewers when they encounter European historical painting. Today its repertoire of gestural rhetoric and its use of warfare as a site for mannered posturings strikes us as inappropriate. This is partly because of appalling nature of modern warfare but also because we no longer understand the complex codes of gestural attitudes.

Certain texts rely upon the implied reader being familiar with certain types of specilised knowledge in order for them to be comprehensible. For instance, one of my minor passions is astronomy, but as soon as a text resorts to mathematical notation, my eyes glaze over and my comprehension level drops dramatically.

Texts may be explicitly made for model readers who occupy a clearly definable group. They may signal this implied reader in a very overt manner. For instance children's literature may utilise large typography and simple syntax, together with limited vocabularies. Often it will incorporate a high percentage of visual material — illustrations — which themselves rest upon a fairly restricted set of visual codes, for example, bright colours, non-realistic or fantasy settings. The very *look* of the text suggests who its implied reader is to be.

Finally we can bring this back to the text you are reading at the moment. The fabric of sentence construction being used in this book on the Visual Arts carries traces of an implied reader. For instance, the use of the pronoun 'you' in that first sentence marks the fact that this book — whether I intended it or not — is addressing someone out there. In fact the 'you' it refers to is a complex construction which comes out of a whole series of decisions and assumptions about who my implied readers should be. On the basis of the decisions about who the 'you' is, the book is then 'aimed' at them.

Whilst visual texts do not and cannot avail themselves of the complex and precise modes of address that are possible in

Are <u>YOU</u> in this?

DESIGNED BY LT. GEN. SIR R. S. S. BADEN-POWELL

35. R. S. S. Baden-Powell *Are you in this?* 1914-18
poster, 77 x 51 cm. (Australian War Memorial, [V5211])

language they can point to their implied readers in some very direct
ways (*see* ill. 35).

These literary studies of the ways in which implied readers are woven into the fabric of texts have had reverberations within the study of the Visual Arts. They have alerted us to the fact that visual texts have as part of their construction ways to address their potential viewers, but beyond this general attribution of addressal or turning they are capable of imagining who their model reader will be with varying degrees of precision.

It would be pleasant to report that each of these three investigations of the nature of Box III was now fixed and all that was required was a great deal of hard work and application in order to produce a unified theory of of the encounter between subject and artistic text. Unfortunately, in the study of the humanities this type of regular progression rarely occurs. What we have seen is that the attempts to move across this new terrain still retain traces of where they set out from. The philosophical investigation was really about how subjects acquire knowledge of the texts they encounter — that is the subject that philosophers are dealing with is the *knowing subject*. The subject in the psycho-analytical approach is not concerned with knowledge but with *the subject of pleasure*. The final cut through the area, that of the implied reader/viewer is concerned how a particular text is able to envisage the desired way it is to be read or viewed.

What is left then is a series of maps which can be overlayed on the area of Box III — maps which do not add up to a unified a coherent plan of the area, but enable the viewer to move through different sets of territories.

The visual text

One difficulty with using the term 'visual text' in an unqualified way is that it appears able to, quite unproblematically, define and describe a set of texts that cluster together naturally. Yet consider the following question.

What are the differences and similarities that pertain between a painting, a novel, and a theatrical performance? From the perspective of sight it could be said that all three engage the eye but in different ways. The painting (at least until the 20th century) represented absent things and people as if they were present. The novel, through the marks on its pages is able to call up in the mind of the reader events and characters. The theatrical performance, through the use of actors, speech and props, is able to present characters, places and events to the audience as if they were really

present. In each case sight and visuality is utilised but differentially.

It has been commonplace amongst some modern artists and
critics to invoke a mythology of *visual exclusivity* for Art History
as a way to mark off its particular distinctiveness. Many 20th
century artists — usually those of a bent towards abstraction, but
not exclusively — have sought to base their aesthetic on such a
notion as that represented in Figure 7.1.

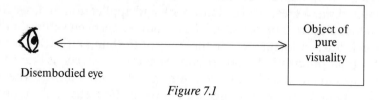

Disembodied eye

Figure 7.1

Thus the encounter between the work and the viewer is thought to
take place in a situation of absolute and autonomous visual perception. There are a number of variants on this model. The work
may be thought of as nothing more than an object-for-sight. It is
shorn of all extra-perceptual pollution, being an object of pure
visuality. As the USA artist Frank Stella remarked, 'What you see
is what you see'.

The work, through its use of 'basic' line, colour or shape is
capable of leaping the gap between it and its viewer, magically
causing its meaning to be generated in the spectator. Kandinsky
often comes close to this mystical behaviourism.

Alternatively, the eye may be thought of as being stripped of its
surround. In this condition it becomes capable of grasping a pre-
cultural, or non-artifical meaning for the work.

From such Modernist ideas about the specificities of the Visual
Arts has developed a whole set of ideas about what is the appropriate way of looking at works. It is thought that looking is at
its 'purest' when stripped of extraneous elements. Very often this
is thought of as consisting of parrying the influences of language
(story-telling) and the artificialities of modern cultural life. The
more it approaches a supposed state of pure and absolute visuality the more it and its viewer approach its truth. Frequently, this
has been accompanied by making analogies between painting
and music where the abstract, non-referential, qualities of musical sound are thought to have an equivalent in the domains of
sight and visual works of Art. My opening example about the

ubiquitous presence of sight in differing Art forms was used in order to cast doubt on the idea that we can ever reach such an absolute zero of visual perception, but also to suggest that in the Visual Arts it is not a question of a retreat into pure sight which is taking place, but the activation of and engagement with differing modalities of vision.

So works of Art manifest a particular *combination* of forms of visuality that we might term a 'to-be-looked-at-ness'. The viewer, on the other hand activates a particular mode of sight that we might term 'a-looking-at-ness'. I also suspect that both instances rest upon a set of highly coded activities which require a high degree of 'complicity' before any substantial exchanges can take place. The antipathy felt towards much Modern Art is a failure to recognise these qualities in the object, or an inability to classify it as being meaningful — a phrase like 'Rubbish! There's nothing there' is a symptom of this condition. The viewer may be unfamiliar with the etiquettes involved in the activities of looking-at-ness — 'It does nothing for me' or 'I can't see what all the fuss is about'. Either a failure of the object to become visible, or a lack of knowledge of where to stand.

With this established we need to move on and consider precisely what visual modalities are required for an encounter to occur.

The edge
One of the fundamental characteristics of a visual image is that it has an edge, that it stops. Unlike 'reality' which appears as unbounded, the image constantly displays to its viewer the fact that it is different from 'reality' by having an edge. It is this basic characteristic which signals that it is an image and therefore is coded. It says, 'I am to be looked at in a particular way' and in so doing marks itself off as being different from other sights that may come into view. Without a frame or edge it would be impossible for us to detect the object as being different, so the presence of an edge indicates that what is in view is to be looked at by a different set of rules. Of course, the presence of this edge has repercussions beyond the frame. For instance, in those media which are ubiquitous in the modern world — say television — where they form a constant accompaniment to daily life the edge may be porous such that the domains of inside and outside became blurred. (The 'outside' may undergo a process of 'televisualisation' and we may look at it as if it were inside.) It is also the case that the rules for looking

at images are able to seep into other areas and the modalities of vision which are particularised around images get applied to such things as landscape, sunsets or urban decay. Such phenomena become 'picturesque', that is they are regarded as having the qualities of to-be-looked-at-ness. There is no 'pure' visuality anywhere rather viewers constantly shift in a horizontal fashion across different sets of 'looking-at-ness'.

When confronted with an image such as *Pegwell Bay* (ill. 34, p. 129) we know that it is an image (it has edges) but we also know that it is a 'life-like' depiction at the same time. Both operate simultaneously. How we see it and what we are seeing are the outcome of *synthesis* of at least two ways of seeing. We *see* the beach and the chalk cliffs, we see the setting sun and the receding tide, and we *see* the figures spaced out across the surface of the image, in a very particular way. They are both what they appear to be but they are also components within an image — they are inside the edge. This means that we are also engaging with the qualities of imageness. The organisation of the figures in relation to one another only have a meaning in terms of where they are placed in relation to that edge. The field of looks created by the differing degrees that the figures are turned towards or away from us are meaningful only in relation to that fifth edge, the picture plane through which we look. The laterality of the image formed by the cliffs and the reefs of exposed rock are only lateral in terms of the top and bottom edges of the picture. The way of seeing engaged with in an image such as *Pegwell Bay* is neither a simple recognition of 'real things' nor an act of pure visuality where we see nothing *but* lines, shapes or colours (a pure visual image) but is the synthesis of *both* registers of looking.

Although the work of Malevich is still elusive Art Historians generally believe that one aspect of his Suprematist work was concerned with the artist's vision of a utopian future (ill. 36). This was a world of pure relations — social, economic, and spiritual — and such works as these were a type of visual mnemonic — directed to a future rather than a past — by which the viewers would be able to imagine or envision what this perfect world might be like. Unlike our previous example there is no question of an oscillation between recognition of elements from outside the frame and a consideration of the object as a purely visual entity. The former has lessened, although there are still traces of this as indicated by the title, it is the latter dimension of the imageness of the object

36. Kasimir Malevich: *Suprematist Composition: Airplane Flying* 1914. Oil
on canvas, 58.1 x 48.3 cm
(Collection, The Museum of Modern Art, New York)

which is being stressed. This is not a retreat into a perceptual
purity of looking, but there is an intensification of the significance
of the edge in that the viewer is being told in a coded way that the
quality of *being-looked-at-ness* is to be engaged with before anything else. The edge in this painting is more like an abyss between
inside and outside since the outside, the referent of the painting,
does not yet exist.

The varieties of visual readings

We must now consider some of the major ways in which we *read* visual images.

The pleasures of the gaze

Return to the disembodied eye and our object of pure visuality (Fig. 7.1, p. 148).

Perhaps the most damning criticism of such a conception as Figure 7.1 is that the 'disembodied eye' and the 'object of pure visuality' simply does not exist. The eye/vision has to be seen as a unit of the whole viewer both mentally and physically. Reversing the relationship in this figure would turn the Art work into something that was indifferent to the physical make up of the viewers and their location within a set of social relations. It is in psycho-analysis that we will find a sustained consideration of where sight, and in particular the relationships between the see-er and the seen, rests in the development of the mature adult.

Recent work within psycho-analysis has been at pains to show that the situations in which we encounter artistic texts can be thought of in terms of the ways in which all of our relations with external objects are constructed. That is our relations to artistic texts are drawn into the ways our instincts develop and are altered as we make the progression from infant to adult, or from nature to the domain of culture and the world of social relations. What Freud tried to explore was the fact that the infant experiences *successive* modes of relating to the external world via the various orifices of the body. The most famous of these relations is that of the mouth and the mother's breast together with the sensations of extreme pleasure, pain, peace and anxiety that are carried in this relationship. There are two other orifices — the eyes — those holes in the head through which and out of which a variety of pleasur-able/unpleasurable transactions can take place.

One of the crucial phases which an infant has to go through is the transition from an hallucinatory state to one where dreaming and perception of the 'real' world become separate and distinct. This is the point where, theoretically, people are able to distinguish between a dream state and being awake, of being able to recognise that what we are seeing on the screen of our dreams is distinct from that which we see before our eyes. Freud always stressed that the adult's ability to discriminate between the two conditions was always a tentative balancing act. Moments of extremity or the presence of certain sorts of objects could always shift the divisions we make such that the principles of the dream world could migrate across into our waking lives. On the screen of our dreams and in our waking lives we continually encounter attempts by the unconscious to insinuate itself into our relations with objects. What was at stake in such overspills or insistencies was the securing of our earlier, infantile feelings of pleasure (the erotic) or the avoidance of pain (anxieties, phobias).

Here an analogy between the line, or edge, between dreaming and wakefulness to the frame or edge of a visual image can be used — or for that matter the edge of the cinema screen or the proscenium arch surrounding a stage. It may be that in looking at an image we are permitted to shift the normal boundaries between the real and the dream, or what is more likely, move into a realm intermediate between the two.

All that psycho-analysis is claiming here is that all human subject/object relations never totally 'forget' either their origins within the first forms that such exhanges took place or the stages that these relations go through as we progress towards adulthood. Looking and sight, being itself a type of subject/object relation partakes, in various ways, in this 'remembering'.

But psycho-analysis goes much further than this and claims that the erotic component of vision may be located in *the varieties of relationships* that can be established between the subject and object. It is in the transactions *between* these two poles that we should be looking. In terms of sight this gives us an active and a passive mode.

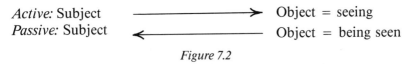

Active: Subject ⟶ Object = seeing
Passive: Subject ⟵ Object = being seen

Figure 7.2

These two relationships are eroticised by psycho-analysis into the pleasures of *voyeurism* and the pleasures of *exhibitionism*.

Our relationships with visual images rarely manifest themselves in such simple ways because subject (viewer) and object (image) are capable of switching roles. Our relationship becomes more like 'I look, but I am looked at'. This is most intense when the image contains a pair of eyes which looks back at us, but something like this is always present because the bounded or framed image, by displaying the quality of 'to-be-looked-at-ness' is in fact throwing back the look of the viewer to its point of origin. Put another way, we might say that the picture is in my eye, but I am in the picture.

An illustration from everyday life will make these complexities clearer. Often going to a party involves dressing up in a particular set of clothes. We like to wear outfits that will look attractive and enhance our appearance. What we are doing is, in fact, preparing ourselves as a sight, turning ourselves into a trap for the look of others. But this preparation, the clothes, the posture, haircuts, and other preenings also throws back the look of the person seeing us because it is an ensemble which has the look of the other person built into its very fabric. Party clothes speak both of being looked at and of looking. In this they closely resemble Figure 7.3.[1]

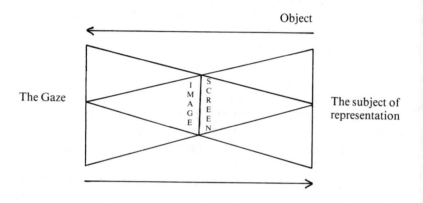

Figure 7.3

Visual images are rather like objects in their party clothes since they are both traps for the look of their viewer as well as texts which have the look of their viewer built into them. This presence of the viewers look constitutes their essence of imageness. The viewer is their *voyeur* at one moment and their seen at another, whilst the image is *exhibitionist* and looker.

This form of psycho-analytic approach differs greatly from the more notorious version that scrutinises the image for sexual symbolism — towers are declared 'phallic', caves and entrances are declared uterine. The type of approach outlined above is more concerned with the general conditions of looking, at the types of transactions that occur between viewer and image and the ways in which such transactions contain echoes of childhood, rather than with the mechanical application of checklists of sexual symbolism. An approach like the former enables us to understand a great many aspects of visual imagery in a more subtle way. For instance looking may take on a particularly voyeuristic mode, it may become inquisitorial, desirous of exploring an image for its 'secrets'. The transparency of the fourth wall of stage-set image organisation allows the look of the viewer to pass through the paint and into the scene beyond. Other images may utilise the painted surface to throw veils across the image subjecting the look to a pleasurable delay. Particular angles of vision, soft focus, or various blocking devices may increase the pleasures of voyeurism by creating the illusion of being a hidden looker, of seeing but not being seen. Still other images may turn their surfaces into an exhibitionist riot and by a brilliant display of line and colour hold the viewers' look in its dazzling patterns.

Thus images may engage their viewer through a variety of strategies. Subtle invitations, sensual strip-tease, diversionary tactics or pyrotechnic exhibitions. In each case it is the ways in which sight is played with, that constitute the pleasures of both looking and being looked at.

Looking for knowledge and looking for pleasure

It is now time to consider the more specific properties of a visual image and of its constituent components, visual codes, because there are a number of properties which differentiate them from other coded forms. What are the properties of visual codes?

Visual codes are primarily codes which are deployed in *space*. That is we normally see all the elements of visual image simultaneously. (Unlike the linguistic signs of speech or music, which are deployed through time.) Thus all the elements of a visual package of information are encountered at 'one hit'. There appears to be a strong tendency to read visual signs in a mimetic fashion, that is to relate visual signs to 'real' objects. The predominance of a set of simultaneous, spatially deployed visual signs does not mean that there are no *internal* relations, or processes within a visual image, rather that such relations and processes are at work within the more general unit of information of 'This is an image', part of its quality of to-be-looked-at-ness. It is true that the relation between the visual sign and the object it represents is generally one of resemblance (unlike the word), but it is also the case that within works of Art — and perhaps all visual images — we are also permitted to look at the image in another way. We can look at the visual sign in terms of its *aesthetic qualities* as well as in terms of its properties of resemblance.

The conclusion is that the visual sign has a tendency to split in two directions according to the priorities brought to it by its potential viewer. It is the presence of the edge, or spatial bounded-ness, which permits both or one type of looking to be activated. When confronted by an image such as Manet's (ill. 37) it is not a matter of simply 'Looking at it', rather that our look is 'switched' along different tracks according to our hierarchy of priorities. For instance I have seen this painting reproduced in a volume entitled *Five Thousand Years of Fashion*. The citation of the painting (artist's name and painting title) was accompanied by the following sentence.

> Even in the eighteen hundreds children's clothes were still modeled on those of adults, bulky and not very practical.[2]

'Looking' here, is scrutinising the visual signs of the painting in terms of their resemblance to the objects they are representing.

37. Edouard Manet: *Gare Saint-Lazare* 1873
(National Gallery of Art, Washington)

Extraction of knowledge — in this case about French women's fashions of the 1880s — is its final aim. It is as if this operation can only be successful to the extent that the look 'sees through' the paintingness of the image. However, when the Manet painting was reproduced in a monograph devoted solely to his work it had a very different text:

> Despite the title, the picture is only slightly involved with urban reality. It is clearly a studio painting and its individuality depends upon the play of the flatly painted figures against the severe grid of the railings.[3]

It is clear that in the second instance a different type of 'looking' is being engaged with. It is one where the resemblance or mimetic relationships of the image are being downgraded — 'the picture is only slightly involved with urban reality' — and instead we are being invited to see it as primarily as an aesthetic object. In each instance a different register of looking is being deployed.

It was noted earlier that because of the predominantly spatial nature of the visual sign and the visual image, there was a propensity in the viewer to read the visual text as being a mimetic space. That is to see the physical marks within the edge as standing in for (representing) physical objects that were 'off-stage'. If one does not ask too many searching questions about this mimetic propensity then it is a short step for the viewer to adopt a mode of looking which examines the image in terms of the information that can be extracted about the world it purports to represent. This is particularly strong when the 'world' of the image has passed away. Thus visual images can be seen as historical documents, valuable traces of past worlds which enable us to reconstruct what life was like. Such operations can only happen if it is assumed that the visual sign or image matches the objects it is representing.

It would be foolish to assert that *no* historical information can be extracted from visual images, it can. However, I suspect that what this historical/informational mode of looking is best at is to generate an understanding of how images were constructed in the past, rather than extracting secure knowledge of the details of past ways of life.

What of the aesthetic reading? In a way this is the exact opposite of the historical or informational reading in that it places the reading within a set of parameters which de-historicise the very act of interpretation. We return to our *disembodied eye*. A pure perceptual interaction or field is posited between an image's formal properties and an universal eye. What is overlooked in this is that the set of options for viewing a visual text — the informational and the aesthetic — is itself the outcome of a set of historical processes. It is not that the aesthetic mode of looking is 'wrong', rather that it seems to be able to operate in a situation where it represses/forgets that it is itself historically located. It is neither a pure act of seeing nor a 'natural' response but a very particular — and modern — way of decoding a visual text.

1   This diagram appears in Jacques Lacan *The Four Fundamentals of Psycho-Analysis* London: Penguin, 1979, p. 106.
2   Mila Contini *Five Thousand Years of Fashion* Milan: Chartwell Books Inc., 1979, pp. 126-7.
3   Nicholas Wadley *Manet* London: Hamlyn, 1967, p. 38.

8

The role of mediation or looking from somewhere

In the preceding section I have attempted to establish the more general aspects of the encounter between text/viewer. However, when we begin to introduce this simple model to the full richness of the aesthetic circuit it becomes much more complex.

A text always presents itself to a viewer from a somewhere. That is the Art object (even in the form of a reproduction) will always be encountered in a concrete situation, be it room, gallery, on a wall, a somewhere.

We must now turn our attention to the *place* in which the viewer encounters the image and the ways in which this can affect the processes of image decoding.

Mediation in general

Returning to the relations operating between Box I and Box II we are now aware that the process of coding involves the producer assembling or re-activating a number of elements — the signs and codes — in order to produce a symbolic object. We will call this stage *primary coding* — a process whereby the artist produces a text which can have a precise meaning or at least move between certain desired limits. We will call the aim of primary coding *the preferred meaning* of the work. Here the artists are the arbiters of this preferred meaning. But as we have seen it is in the nature of texts to shift across a varying set of meanings, particularly when the source of the preferred meaning, the artist, is no longer available to provide the spectator with a work's definitive meaning.

Between boxes II and III a process of *secondary coding or mediation* can take place and this can deflect or totally transform the nature of the preferred meaning.

To illustrate the nature of mediation I will use an example taken from architecture. One of the key buildings in the story of modern European architecture is the Fagus Factory, built by Walter Gropius and Adolf Meyer in Germany in 1911 (*see* ill. 38). I have conducted tutorials on the position which this building occupies in the Modern Movement. As I have never visited the factory I have had to rely upon slides and photographic views reproduced in the standard works of Architectural History. In almost every instance the building is photographed from a particular position and selects the same element to highlight. It is always the facade which is depicted, presumably because it is here that one encounters the most modern stylistic elements — the use of glass, cubic form, and the unclad corners. But there are other less modern aspects of the building (*see* ill. 39). Which of these two photographs most 'truthfully' illustrates the Fagus Factory? The answer is both. However, if one had to rely solely upon photographs it would be the one which occurs most frequently. (In this case ill. 38.) The result is that the most commonly occurring depictions eventually 'stand in' for the whole building and thereby effect the significance they have for the viewer.

These two photographs can be seen as elements of *secondary encoding* in that they mediate between the factory and the viewer. The factory depicted in each of these photographs does not differ in its physical dimension or in its material construction but through the process of mediation it can appear differently and therefore mean different things to the viewer. Mediation then refers to the processes whereby meanings are transmitted from one point to another. The crucial thing is that such agencies of mediation are not passive mediums which carry an original set of meanings to their destination unscathed, they can be active, capable of making radical interventions into the sense which the decoders make of a text.

Mediation in the Visual Arts

Titles
To begin this examination of the processes of mediation we will look at the *title* of a work. Throughout this book I have referred to illustrations and examples in two ways. Wherever possible

38. Front view, Fagus Factory, Altfield, 1911.
Walter Gropius and Adolf Meyer

39. Rear view, Fagus Factory, Altfield, 1911.
Walter Gropius and Adolf Meyer

a reproduction of the work has been included along with the supplementary information of its title, the artist, and its date of completion. You have in your possession then two sets of information — a reproduction of the work and a title. Under 'normal' operating conditions these two pieces of information will be in a close relation so close that it is impossible to separate them, as in the statement 'That is "The Bathers" by Courbet'. As a corollary of this, one set of information can stand in for the other. Almost always it is the title — the words — which substitute for the image. This simple exchange of title for image hides the degree to which we are dependent upon the title for our initial grasping of the work. The title of an image becomes the first mediation that the work is subjected to. Most of you have perhaps been the victims of an experiment beloved by Art History teachers where a work is displayed with the real title being withheld, or with a different title substituted. In the absence of this crucial piece of information visual images are capable of sliding across a wide range of meanings. Despite the desire of much Modern Art to banish the codes of language from the visual image, our dependence upon titles continues unabated. We expect there to be a particular and fixed relation between image and title. Normally it is placed underneath the image and is thought to describe what is in the work, or somehow gives us a summary of its content.

René Magritte was one artist who attempted to disturb this relationship between image and title. Magritte realised it was impossible to banish language from the image and proceeded to take the question of a work's title to the core of what he was doing. He broke with the idea of the title being a description or summary of the picture.

In *Hegel's Holiday* (ill. 40) Magritte has altered the normal operating relationships between the image and its title. Rather than image and title being substitutable for one another, the image and its title are now equal elements. The situation now becomes representable by the simple equation:

$$image + title = work.$$

This simple shift places us in a vertiginal condition where we are no longer certain as to what comes first — image or title — or even whether we should regard either as being potentially translatable into its other element.

Even where the artist is aware of this insinuation of language

40. René Magritte: *Hegel's Holiday* 1958
(Courtesy of Phototheque René Magritte Art Resource)

into the visual image it is difficult to break with it absolutely. Some contemporary artists have opted for giving their works numbers instead of linguistic titles. The difficulty with such a strategy is that the coded language of numbers is not neutral but carries with it a set of associations with mathematics, science, impersonality, and coolness. These associations inevitably migrate across to the work leaving numbered footprints which mediate the viewer's interpretation.

Frames

The *physical presentation* of a work can also mediate its relation to the viewer. In Western art the convention of framing — for instance placing an image within an ornate gilt frame — produces associations of age, importance, and 'old masterishness'. This then moves the object towards the category of a precious luxury item. In turn this re-categorisation may alter the cultural place thought appropriate for the work; it may shift from being a utilitarian object and become a luxury 'Art' item. There are fashions in framing and a great deal of Contemporary Art attempts to mark itself off from these associations by reducing the visibility of the frame or by adopting materials which carry other types of association. Using straightforward wooden frames may imply a desire for simplicity, authenticity or 'craftness'. Modern industrial materials such as steel — much favoured for holding Art photographs — imply Modernity, or Utilitarian Functionalism. The materials used in the frame, particularly the use of precious materials such as gold leaf and jewels were often a way of signifying the esteem in which the image was held. Religious icons are an example, as well as the social status of the powerful figures depicted in portraiture.

Before photographic images were cheap and easily affordable (and even after this) they were placed in ornate frames to indicate either the aspirations of their owners — poor man's paintings — or to signify the intimate and emotional relationship the owner had to the person photographed. Photographs placed within lockets often aped the frames of the earlier forms such as miniatures. In such cases it is likely that the memories of the loved ones would include the frames in which they were set in much the same way that family photographs also call up a memory of their place — the family album.

I suspect that the various framing devices used in European Art played a much more significant mediatory role than we now imagine and were important elements in establishing for the viewer certain general rules about what it was that one was looking at. No one who has visited an old theatre can ignore the degree to which the ornate proscenium arches (frames) were integral to the comprehension of the spectacles that were staged in such buildings. Nor was it by chance that a great deal of interchange took place between the theatrical devices of framing and the devices used in the Visual Arts. In both cases the frame around the image/scene was important in suggesting to the viewer that they were in the presence of certain types of illusionary space.

With sculpture, the cultic origins of the objects have left their traces in the plinths and niches which persisted long after these religious functions had disappeared. One only has to think of the supporting paraphernalia deployed in commemorative sculpture and war memorials to see how easily these archaic framing devices can be pressed back into service in the present day.

The mediatory processes initiated by framing devices operate to encode the space in which the object is placed. Frames provide the viewer with a set of very general signals as to *where* they should imagine the object residing in relation to the other objects, that is they mark it off as being a particular kind of object, inhabiting a particular kind of space. Such devices — again at a general level — may suggest to the viewers the status of the view or scene which they are witnessing.

The museum

If we pursue the theme of *encoded space* as a crucial mediator of a work's meaning, then *where* we encounter an object will be an important element in determining *how* we encounter it. This 'where' will enter into the interpretation that is made of the work. In the contemporary situation it is the *museum* which plays a major role in organising our conceptions of what is and what is not an Art object.

A museum is a fine example of an encoded space which specialises in owning, housing, displaying and interpreting Art objects. Museums, in their modern form, have not always existed. Previously they resembled collections, in the literal sense, but were not regarded as being the very particular sorts of physical and cultural environments that they are now. I want to suggest that museums and art galleries operate in ways very similar to framing devices, alerting us to the fact that we are in a physical environment in which we are likely to encounter Art objects. This sets in train a very complex set of attitudes, assumptions, and behaviours which are thought to be appropriate to the viewing of such objects. One of the reasons for the decline in framing devices for individual works may be that the building in which the objects are housed has itself taken on this role.

Placing an object not normally seen in the context of a museum can radically alter the meaning which it has for us, for instance exhibitions of everyday, utilitarian objects re-frames them as 'aesthetic objects' and this then influences the more general set of attitudes which we adopt towards them. Certain artists in the 20th century have been aware of this museum effect and have incorporated it into their work. Marcel Duchamp was inordinately fond of shuttling objects back and forth across different cultural spaces to see how the meaning of the things changed. Duchamp's most notorious gesture was to enter a urinal purchased from a plumber's shop in the Independent Artists Exhibition held in New York in 1917 (*see* ill. 1, p. 16). He also advocated a reverse move — 'use a Rembrandt as an ironing-board'.

Others have become dissatisfied with the rather reverent mood of places such as museums and have attempted to situate their works in the more robust environments of everyday life. An example is the community Muralist Movements which grew up in the 1970s.

Some years ago I visited an exhibition being staged in an old postal sorting office. On the floor of the building were painted a number of white squares indicating where mailbags were to be deposited for various destinations. During the night a cleaner had swept the floor and placed the litter in one the white squares. When the exhibition opened the following day a number of people were contemplating the neat pile of sweepings. Several were searching in vain for the title card of the work.

Into the museum: discourse

If the nature of the space where the work is shown can mediate its meaning at a general level, then *how* it is displayed *within* that space can penetrate into the very core of the work and utterly transform what we see. In order to show how these sorts of mediation work it is necessary to introduce the theoretical concept of *discourse*.

I have suggested that mediation or secondary coding was not a passive bearer of meaning but was itself active, capable of re-ordering a text into a new set of meanings or laying onto a text an additional set of meanings.

In Art exhibitions it is usual for a short statement to be placed on the wall near the starting point of the show. This statement, often originating from the curator or organiser of the exhibition, introduces the artist and the works displayed and attempts to place them within Art History.

Some years ago I visited an exhibition of works by the English artist William Hogarth (1697-1764). In this exhibition Hogarth was spoken of as 'a great satirist and a man of radical political views'. Some years later I encountered yet another exhibition by this artist, but here he was talked about as being 'a great example of English Art'. His paintings were described as being the 'most intense expression of Englishness'. In both cases the works were being placed within a much wider set of ideas and therefore being framed within a wider set of meanings. This wider set of frameworks we can call *a discourse* in that it is a way of speaking about the pictures and transforming these into texts. By entering into a discourse the 'pictures-as-texts' were made to connect with other discourses. In the case of Hogarth they were inserted into a radical political discourse or became components of a discourse about painting and Englishness. Discourses, then, resemble complex stories or narratives, but they differ from 'story stories' in that they are made up not just of words, but can include words, pictures, and buildings as well as human actions. It is possible — and likely for a building such as an Art gallery or a museum — to be part of a discourse. One only needs to compare the architectural styles of museums in the late 19th century with those of the present day to see that contained within the bricks and mortar or concrete and glass used to make them are concepts about what it is that the buildings are supposed to be doing. We might say that the works of Art are continually being incorporated into 'the big pictures' which are the discourses and these discourses operate at every level of the display and presentation of works of Art.

Exhibitions
Under contemporary viewing conditions we rarely encounter Art works as isolated and autonomous entities. Regular visitors to commercial galleries or publicly funded museums mostly see works as part of a wider grouping, that of the exhibition. This may appear to be a natural way of looking at Art objects but it is in fact a highly conventionalised practice. As always, History shows that things have not always been like this.

As can be seen from illustration 41 even up until the middle of

41. William Powell Frith: The Private View at the Royal Academy, 1881.
Exhibited at the Royal Academy, 1883. *(copyright is reserved by the owner)*

the 19th-century exhibitions of Art works were hung according to
different principles than today. The model upon which such hang-
ing practices rested emerged in the 17th and 18th centuries where
the model was the *cabinet of curiosities.* Here the aim was to display as many items of a collection at once and so paintings might
be hung in such a manner as to overlap one another. In the 19th-
century salon exhibitions huge numbers of works were displayed
simultaneously and the walls of the exhibiting galleries would be
covered from floor to ceiling. It was only towards the end of the
century that works were hung in relative isolation from one
another with the onset of the idea of an Art work as independent
aesthetic entity.

Unlike the 19th-century salons exhibitions, the Modern Art
show is rarely an arbitrary grouping together of works. The hang-
ing of works is usually premised on their being a set of internal
connections between the works. An examination of such pre-
sumed connections will reveal the ideas and assumptions that have
determined how and why that particular set of works has been
hung together.

If there are decisions being made about what is to be included in
an exhibition, there are also decisions being made about what
order the works should be placed in. One of the most elementary
features of an exhibition is the fact that we experience a single
work *in relation* to all the others in the show. Exhibitions are really
a 'package' of Art objects involving a set of decisions on the part
of the curator as to what is the optimum conjunction of the works

to best illustrate the interpretation being mounted. Of course, it is always open to the visitor to violate this curatorial ordering and thread one's own particular pathway through the exhibition space. If this strategy is adopted then it is possible to come away with a different set of relations between the works than those preferred by the organisers, although this form of alternative viewing is often severely limited by the floor plans of the show.

The element of discourse intersects with an exhibiton in that it is from discourse that the various ways of imparting unified meanings to a body of works are drawn. Discourse then, resembles *a fund* of such narratives around which art objects can be *organised*. Put simply discourses are the organisational principles which are employed to impart meanings to the works. We can observe the operations of such discourses by examining the most common forms taken by art exhibitions.

Thematic exhibitions
Such exhibitions may attempt to show how a particular theme or object has been depicted over a given historical period. For instance, 'Wollongong 1888 to 1988'. In such instances the unity of the exhibition derives from something external to the history of the Art itself, so that concerns about the 'quality' of the works may be marginalised in favour of whether they contain an appropriate content.

Group shows
This form of exhibition is commonly used to give young artists their first chance to show their work and hopefully make a sale. But it may be used by the curator/organiser as an opportunity to argue that there is a unity within the works. The claim may be made that the works were selected because it was felt that there were a set of common stylistic or thematic concerns. Such claims may then prompt the visitor to confirm or disagree with such arguments, thus establishing a 'frame' for their inspection.

Historical exhibitions
Here works from the past will be brought together to perform an Art Historical function. There may be an attempt to argue that a particular set of influences were impinging upon the artists of a particular place and time — 'Paris-Sydney: 1900-1925' — or that past interpretations about certain art works were wrong — 'Sydney

Nolan: a case for Reconsideration'. In such exhibitions there is usually an overt recognition on the part of the curator that they are engaged in historical disputation. Again, once the grounds upon which the exhibition has been mounted are exposed it is difficult for the viewer to 're-frame' the works to other ends.

Solo exhibitions, retrospectives
These exhibitions are normally staged as a way of acknowledging that artists having reached their artistic maturity and that the time has arrived to review their work as a whole. By gathering a large body of their work together in a single place it is hoped that a 'clearer' view may emerge. The discursive unity operating here is usually the lives of the artists themselves, that is the work is reviewed in the light of the life. Or there may be an attempt to detect the existence of an overarching developmental sequence or thematic consistency. The assumption in both instances is that such unities in the life or the work are locatable and it would be hard to imagine how such exhibitions might be organised if instead of biographical unity only fragmentation and disunity were to be found.

International exhibitions
With the increasing internationalisation of the Art market has gone an increasing internationalisation of Art images; Art personnel, and Art debates. Originally part of the World Trade Exhibitions that emerged towards the end of the 19th century, international art shows are now firmly fixed as part of the Art calendar. (The most famous are perhaps the Biennale's held in Venice, Sydney, and São Paulo and the contemporary 'Art Fair' held at Kassel in West Germany.) There is still a great deal of controversy concerning such Art events although one thing is clear to anyone who has visited them. Rather than being *international*, such events are the places where Art nationalism is raised to its most intense level. Works of Art take on the function of national flags.

All exhibitions, either consciously or unconsciously, by drawing on the unities and narratives contained within discourses, mediate the works to their viewers. All exhibitions, of necessity, submit the works to secondary codings.

Discourse becomes the Museum

So far, the discussion about mediation has been limited to the ways in which discourses are folded into the internal organisation of the museum to produce various types of coded space. However, the museum can embody discourses and become an argument in bricks and mortar.

Perhaps the most influential museum of the 20th century is the Museum of Modern Art (MOMA)[1] in New York. It opened in 1929 and because it was one of the first Art museums to specialise in collecting Modern Art. Located in the largest city in USA, it quickly became extraordinarily influential — it was a paradigm — for how Modern Art should be exhibited.

The Museum's permanent collection is housed on the second and third floors of the building. The ground plans are reproduced in order to help you follow the story which the organisation of the exhibits is 'speaking' (*see* figs 8.1, 8.2).

The narrative embodied in the Museum rests upon a number of assumptions about the history of Modern Art.

- French painting (with both of those terms being stressed) is the core of the Modernist Movement in the Visual Arts
- the high points of the story — its major stages — are most clearly evident in the 'best' works of a few 'major' artists
- Modern Art is conceived as moving in an evolutionary manner. A → B → C → D. These are the 'isms' of Modernism and they are to be thought to consist of clusters of stylistic innovation, each one 'extending and developing' the 'breakthroughs' achieved by its predecessor

The point is that these are assumptions unspoken and taken as self-evident.

A visitor to these floors of the Museum is guided through a particular version of Art History; there is the central narrative thread which on the second floor is the succession 1/2/3/4/5/6/7/8/9/10/11/12/13/14. The detours or 'dead ends' are Architecture and Design, and the early North Americans, the Latin Americans and the 'Primitives'. On the third floor the detours from the main story are photography, drawings and prints and the whole of Modern Sculpture! The sequence/succession in which the rooms are visited is meant to represent a succession of *historical causes*.

According to MOMA, the history of modern art begins with Cezanne who confronts you at the entrance to the permanent collection . . . he foreshadows Picasso and Cubism, from Picasso

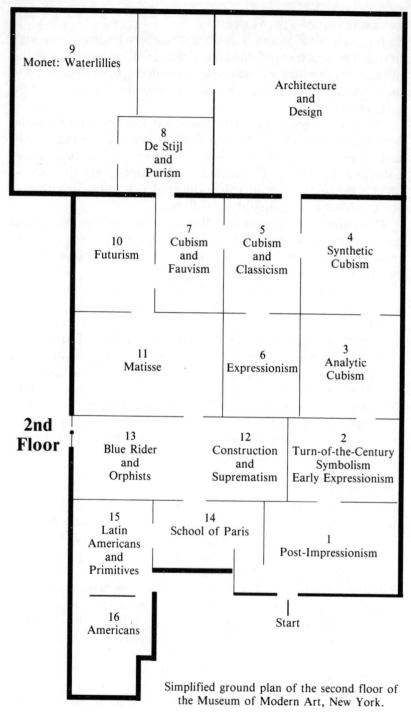

Simplified ground plan of the second floor of the Museum of Modern Art, New York.

Figure 8.1

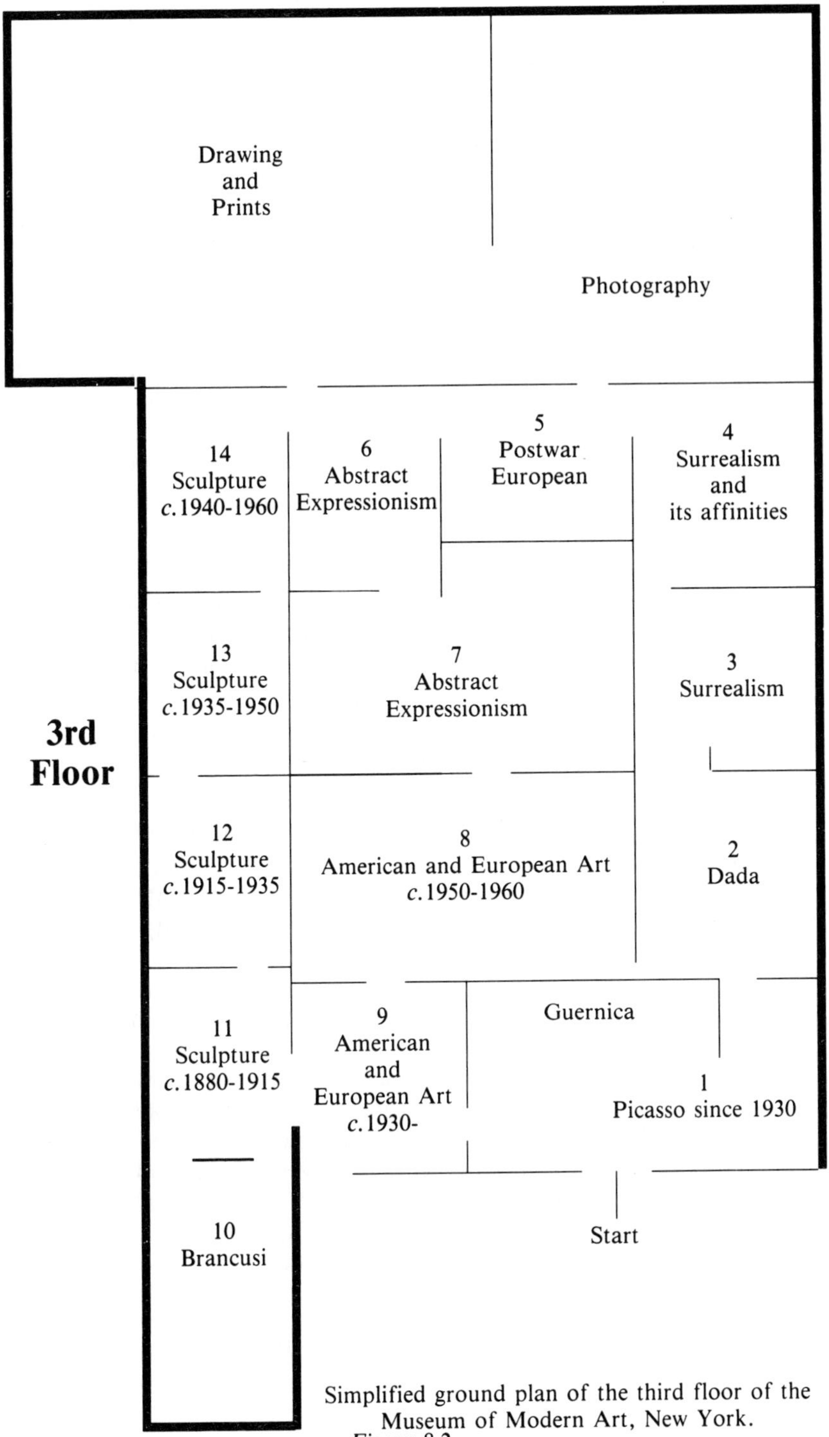

Drawing and Prints

Photography

14
Sculpture
c.1940-1960

6
Abstract
Expressionism

5
Postwar
European

4
Surrealism
and
its affinities

13
Sculpture
c.1935-1950

7
Abstract
Expressionism

3
Surrealism

12
Sculpture
c.1915-1935

8
American and European Art
c.1950-1960

2
Dada

11
Sculpture
c.1880-1915

9
American
and
European Art
c.1930-

Guernica

1
Picasso since 1930

10
Brancusi

Start

3rd
Floor

Simplified ground plan of the third floor of the
Museum of Modern Art, New York.
Figure 8.2

and Cubism issue almost everything else: Leger, the Futurists, the Constructivists . . . on the third floor the mainstream recommences with *Guernica* . . . after Picasso, Miro is presented as the prototypical surrealist.[2]

From this point a smooth sequential flow is established from Surrealism to Abstract Expressionism, which is made to appear as the logical fulfilment of the whole of Modern Art.

We can also examine the internal organisation of the Australian National Gallery. When it opened in 1982 a flurry of articles appeared in the press and Art journals. Those adopting a critical approach to the building and its internal organisation all focused on the fact that it embodied a view of Art and Art History that was inappropriate to Australia, utilising a view of Modern Art that was outdated and which rested upon that formulated by the Museum of Modern Art.

The most incisive of these criticisms were those advanced by David Bromfield[3] whose argument rests upon two points. Firstly that it is the art of the Abstract Expressionists of New York which is made the focal point of the Gallery, but as Bromfield states, it is dubious whether this art does in fact deserve this privileged position within the Australian context. Canberra is not New York and the Australian National Gallery is not MOMA. Secondly by combining a masterpiece view of Art with an evolutionary model of artistic change and then building these assumptions into the very structure of the permanent exhibitions, the Museum stops visitors exercising their *own* choices. Bromfield gives us a telling example of how this internal organisation can establish implicit relations between the works —

> Because Claude Monet painted very large images of his waterlily pool, it was according to this view, inevitable that Mark Rothko would make his large stained canvasses of blocks of colour and that Jackson Pollock would produce his enormous tangle of gestures *Blue Poles* . . . To walk through the major galleries is somewhat like turning the pages of a cheap American paperback of art history. One comes to the Monet waterlilies and then the Pollock. There is no other way around the building. It has been designed to force you to see things 'this way'.[4]

These two examples make it clear, I think, that museums are not simply hangars for Art works. They are framing devices in which a coded space becomes a set of public discourses upon Art. As such they are capable of producing quite particular and concrete arguments about the nature of the objects which live inside them.

Within the modern Art museum two types of mediatory process finally collide and begin to merge. The first is a tendency for the museum to expand its functions beyond that of housing Art objects to becoming an embodiment of cultural discourses, a unit of encoded space. The increasing flexibility of exhibition environments has meant that there is a greater potential for them to take on the form of the discourses which the curator/organiser of the show is bringing to bear on the works. The second tendency is for the works to be increasingly integrated into a set of discursive narratives generated within the ancillary institutions of the Art world (to be examined in the next section). On both counts the works undergo a more intense form of secondary coding.

Many artists, writers and critics have bemoaned this move, seeing it as a violation of the essentially *visual component* of the Visual Arts. Dissatisfaction on this score has often lead to movements of perceptual fundamentalism, where a Golden Age of visual innocence is posited — a state of being where viewer and work can encounter one another unencumbered by the word. The chief problem with this formulation is that the Golden Age never existed and never will; such 'stripped down' states for encountering Art have always been a fantasy, a dream. The increasing integration of Art works and public discourse are indicative of a complex shift in the social placement of Art that has been gathering momentum since World War II. For instance, there has been a steady rise in educational standards and with it a raising of the intellectual expectations both artists and the public have in relation to Art. The 'blow out' in the investment market for Art has meant an increasing demand for knowledge of the works which such economic interest generates. Finally the increasing professionalisation of careers in Art has led to much greater involvement of artists — as teachers, writers, critics, and administrators — in those public Art discourses which are so often criticised.

In a way what has happened is that Art has returned to a modern variation of an older form. The long Romantic interlude is coming to a close along with the myths about artists and Art making that accompanied it — it is in fact once more becoming a highly integrated cultural activity, an object of interest and anxiety and therefore something appearing to need professional administration.

I have suggested that mediation or secondary encoding was not only something generated by the immediate environment of a work (the title and the frame) or by the museum, but could also be located across numerous other institutions within the Art world. It is to these ancillary institutions that I now want to turn and consider some of the ways in which this circuit can come full circle by looking at the relations between Box I and Box III.

The changes in the organisation of Art already mentioned have led to a great increase in the traffic between viewer and artist and vice versa. It has always existed in a variety of forms — patronage, money, shared assumptions about Art, and common regimes of taste. However, since World War II many more artists are participating in the processes of mediation. They are invited to be the curators of exhibitions; they participate in the activity of writing and criticism; they get seconded onto the boards of museums; they are Arts administrators; they are teachers. Artists now participate in (and bring to the processes of production) a plethora of secondary encodings that are integral to the contemporary Art world. An example from a 1980s catalogue illustrates this:

> This exhibition evolved from an observation by Nottingham artist Chris Tunwell and his colleague Michael Wootton that a new and potent spirit of Critical Realism was currently emerging in the work of diverse artists across Britain and *their suggestion* that the time was ripe for a collective showing of this work.[5]

Here we can see the producers of Art actively engaging in the work of secondary encoding, almost as sub-curators, as they suggest both the theme and the title of the exhibition. This then provides the works with a mediatory unifier within which the various works are exhibited. In this instance the traffic was from Box I to Box III, but the reverse also occurs. The Art critic is pivotal here, not simply as a post-hoc interpreter of the work, but as a figure who can, both literally and metaphorically, stand at the artist's elbow and make 'helpful interpretations'. It is important to bear such exchanges in mind because it would be wrong to understand mediation in terms of the numerous conspiracy theories that circulate in the Art world. Oppositions such as critics versus artists, words versus pictures, teachers versus doers may be satisfying in the short term, but will not stand up for long when the complexity of the actual situation is examined.

The catalogue
In its modern form, the catalogue is perhaps the most obvious point where the mediatory discourses generated beyond the museum are most commonly encountered by the viewer. What is a catalogue and what is its function?

The modern catalogue can range from a single roneoed sheet listing the titles, dates and prices of the works through to the large, book-like volumes which accompany prestigious historical surveys or retrospectives. I will concentrate on the more substantial type of production because it is there that one can see the multiple mediatory functions of the catalogue in their most concentrated form.

It is clear from the 96-page catalogue for the 'Dreams, Fears and Desires' exhibition[6] — mounted in Sydney in 1984 — that it is doing more than providing the viewer with a simple inventory of the works displayed. The title, 'Aspects of Australian Figurative Painting 1942-1962 : Dreams, Fears and Desires' signals the two components of the exhibition. Firstly there is a statement about what is being exhibited:

(a) Australian
(b) Figurative Painting
(c) 1942-1962

This information establishes a set of clear parameters as to what has been chosen to be included *in* the exhibition, as well as to what is being excluded — Australian Non-Figurative Painting/Sculpture 1942-1962. The subtitle supplements this information by suggesting how the work will be interpreted — it will be seen through the lenses of dreams, fears, and desires. Within the title there is an elementary move from *defining* the works to suggesting the direction that interpretation will take. This cross-referencing continues with the cover illustration where the subtitle 'Dreams, Fears and Desires' seeps across to embrace the image below (ill. 42). We cannot but help relate this work to the three words placed above it. The fact that its title 'The Shadow' appears to coincide with the word 'Fears' simply confirms this framing.

The list of works exhibited occurs towards the end of the volume

Aspects of Australian
Figurative Painting
1942–1962

Dreams, Fears and Desires

66 Charles Blackman (b.1928)
    The Shadow, 1953

Christine Dixon and Terry Smith

42. Cover of the catalogue for the 1984 exhibition
(Power Institute of Fine Arts, University of Sydney)

and occupies three pages of the total of ninety-six. The bulk of the publication is taken up by a number of interpretative essays and informative collations. There is an 'Introduction' (pp. 7-18) in which the general mythic themes of the work are mentioned together with an argument which places the work of the period in relation to 'the recent fashionable revival of fifties style'. There is a clear invitation in the closing sentence of the essay to look at the work in the light of the present,

> The timeliness of this work is not simply that there is a renewal of this kind of painting, but that it gives us the opportunity to interrogate such images — both past and present — more critically than we did in the 1950s.[7]

What is important to grasp here is that there is no question of the works simply being assembled and the viewers being left to their own devices. (We have seen that no such innocent encounter is possible.) The catalogue is an avowedly interpretative exercise. In the major curatorial essay (pp. 19-81) the authors signal their interpretative stance by sub-dividing the exhibition into sections. Beneath the word 'Framework' (p. 24) seven sections are identified and these provide a set of subsidiary titles beneath which are arranged the complete works of the exhibition. On pages 66-67 there is a section entitled 'Chronology' which lists year by year (1938-1963) the major global and local events which the authors feel bear upon the conditions under which the paintings were produced. There then follows a discussion of the individual sections of the exhibition (pp. 71-81) and it is here that the works are interpreted in terms of the various thematic unities that the authors are deploying. For instance — 'Marks of Violence I', 'A World of Wars', 'Marks of Violence II: A Wounding of Women', 'Myths of Place I: Still Life in the City', 'Myths of Place II: Empty Centre and Anti-hero', 'Signs of the Other I: Constructions of Childhood', 'Signs of the Other II: White on Black'. The volume ends with a bibliography of books and articles which the authors feel informs their discussion.

I have discussed this particular catalogue because it is important to demonstrate that mediation, in the form of interpretation, is not a sinister exercise undertaken to *brainwash* the viewer. It is an exercise aimed at drawing out meanings from the works. The catalogue, in this form, is a medium through which an active interpretation is conducted. We might summarise this process as follows:

images + language + exhibition space = an argument

Debating Art

Beyond the walls of the museums and Art galleries we begin to encounter the domains of academic Art History and the more general debates about Art that get conducted within the institutions, journals, and magazines that constitute the Art world. Such debates — or disputes about and over meaning — rest upon the work which is produced by those doing advanced research in the study of the Visual Arts. For instance the 'Dreams, Fears and Desires' catalogue was the product of two curators, one a postgraduate student, the other a full-time academic, both of whom are specialists in the field of Australian Art History. When exhibitions are mounted they are often reviewed and talked about in the columns of newspapers or the pages of Art journals and it is here that other viewpoints, criticisms or praise will surface. The 'Dreams, Fears and Desires' exhibition drew a counter response from Professor Bernard Smith, another Art Historian.

Art journals in the 20th century have been particularly powerful mediatory agents for Art debate. Often they will have been established upon a founding manifesto, where the overall project of the magazine or journal will be spelt out by its editor(s). Journals and magazines often set themselves a task to perform, usually in the form of arguing for and giving voice to a set of aesthetic preferences, a set of political values, and a set of cultural positions. To further this end it may utilise writers who are in broad agreement with such aims as well as promoting the work of artists who are thought to best embody the aims and values upon which the project of the magazine rests. Here is an excerpt from the editorial of the first edition of the Australian magazine *Art and Text*.

> *Art and Text* cannot expect, nor does it aspire, to publish work which shares all the above concerns. The Australian critical field is simply not large enough. Neither is this the purpose for which the magazine was initiated. As the content of this first issue demonstrates, a wide variety of critical approaches is worthy of inclusion. Essays by and about Australian and, sometimes, overseas artists, theoretical and cultural analyses, inquiries into the relationships between several arts and an avoidance of extensive interviewing, reviewing and lavish illustrations all aim to establish *Art and Text* as a forum for critical and artistic re-examination and experimentation. By means of such a forum, Australian artists and critics may gain a progressive understanding of their 'role and practical potential'.

We have reached the final stage of mediation and the book you are reading at the moment enters the picture. As the introduction made clear, the content, the ideas and many of the values that have been dealt with so far derive from the author's experience of teaching in Art schools and universities. Teaching is itself a process of mediation. However desirable the utopia of absolute objectivity might appear it is, and always will be, a false hope in a subject such as Art History. Teachers, like everyone else, espouse values which exist within discourses. If teachers operate in the field of the Arts it is also likely that they participate in every one of the mediatory processes we have been examining. They will be, as well as teachers, Arts administrators, museum and gallery advisers, writers of catalogues, authors of articles in Art journals and magazines, writers in their specialised areas of study. The single most important *ethical injunction* they operate under is not not to mediate, but rather to *know*, as far as it is possible, from what position they are undertaking their teaching and be able to spell it out in a clear and lucid manner for their students.

The major points that can be drawn from the above analysis are:

- Mediation, or *secondary coding* of some kind, is always present. It should not be thought of as a conspiracy against the 'true' meaning of a work or of a war in which words are plotting to overthrow images. Mediation is an integral part of the circulation of Art works

- Mediation is an activity which is inseparable from the life of Art objects as texts. Meaning gets layered on meaning, interpretation upon interpretation. Mediation is often combative and may overtly set out to contest an Art object's existing meanings and aim to install itself as the *new* meaning

- The original act of coding by the producer may become lost through time, leaving us with nothing but the history of a work's mediations

- Mediation is always a 'motivated' process, although the particular motivation need not be present at a conscious level. The reason for this is that the agencies of mediation are part of and exist in, a social and cultural world. They must, of necessity, be carriers of particular values or bring values to bear upon the works they are mediating. For instance, a shift in cultural values may usher in new regimes of taste. Victorian

Art was re-configured as being worthy of attention and carrying aesthetic merit by certain cultural tendencies operating in the latter part of the 1960s

- Political values may be mobilised to justify the inclusion/exclusion of a particular work in the canon of Art espoused by official institutions. An example of this would be the ideology of Socialist Realism in the USSR and its subsequent re-formulation under 'glasnost'

- Economic values may be affected by Art works undergoing re-formulation. Their value as commodities may then rise or fall.

1   The analysis of MOMA is drawn from Carol Duncan and Alan Wallach 'Museum of Modern Art as Late Capitalist Ritual: an iconographic analysis' in *Marxist Perspectives*, vol. 1, no. 4, Winter 1978, pp. 28-51.
2   *Ibid.* pp. 35-36.
3   David Bromfield 'Never Mind the Quality' in *National Times* October 10-16th, 1982, pp. 12, 14.
4   *Ibid.* p. 12.
5   *Critical Realism: Britain in the 1980's* Nottingham: Catalogue of the Nottingham Castle Touring Exhibition, 1987, p. 4.
6   Christine Dixon and Terry Smith *Aspects of Australian Figurative Painting, 1942-1962: Dreams, Fears and Desires* Sydney: Power Institute of Fine Arts, 1984.
7   *Ibid.* p. 7.

9
The audiences for Art

In discussing the relationships between the viewer and the text I have so far examined it in terms of the nexus between 'looking-at' and 'being-looked-at' in a 'someway'. Then the factors active in coded space or *mediation* a 'somewhere' was considered. This final chapter is concerned with the nature of a 'someone' and it is to the question of *who* that someone might be that we must now turn.

One of the major factors fuelling this interest in the nature of the encounter between an Art work and a viewer has been a move from critics asserting what *ought* to happen to a consideration of *what did* happen when people encountered Art works. In place of *an ideal unity* in and around the Visual Arts the current tendency is to stress shifting patterns of similarity and difference in the senses made of Art works. As contemporary theorists of culture and social life view the modern scene they do not see an absolute unity, rather similarities and differences in the ways in which the various modern social groups conduct their lives, think and feel, and represent to themselves the worlds they inhabit. In this final chapter I will be concentrating upon the ways in which *the differences* between social groups and social categories can affect the encounters between viewers and visual texts.

We are all aware, in part, of such differences which we mark out and refer to through a variety of behavioural patterns, judgements and moral statements. I live in an inner city suburb of Sydney renowned for its rich mix of social groupings. As I am writing I can both see and hear evidences of such differences. My immediate neighbours are two young white males who have a loose affiliation with the skinhead subculture. Membership of this group demands that one have one's head shaved, wear numerous tattoos and play a very restricted type of rock music extremely loudly. Nearby is an Italian family who have recreated a Mediterranean environment in their backyard where each Sunday — weather permitting — the various branches of the family meet beneath the shade of a grapevine and sit down for the long lunch, Italian style. We who have lived in modern urban areas for any length of time have grown used to negotiating our way through such cultural diversity and are familiar with having to make informed guesses as to where a particular person resides within the social order by interpreting the outward manifestations of group affiliation. Clearly an important element in displaying group membership resides in the objects with which people surround themselves. Objects are values and values become objects. That is, the various elements of colour, materials and objects get combined into things with significance (they are coded). Through the different modalities of fashion, interior decor, tastes in music something not too dissimilar to narratives are constantly being constructed. This recognition that different social groups have different types of culture means that in order to understand the meaning that a particular object has for a particular social group we need to know where that object sits within the wider patterns of meaning to which that group subscribes. This has been a crucial theoretical move and in order to grasp fully its implications we need to make a brief detour into the 19th century.

Certainly since the middle of the 19th century in Europe an important area for thinkers, writers and artists has been the anxiety caused by the knowledge that the culture and Art espoused by the educated and/or prosperous groups in society was specific to that group. The realisation of the restricted nature of this culture was joined to a concern about the sorts of culture that the newly literate classes appeared to be drawn towards. Intellectuals were caught between a culture (their own) which they thought of as good and worthwhile, but which remained élitist in its distribution. Against this was a popular culture, which not to put too fine a point on it, terrified the ruling élites by its vigour, vulgarity and violence. The educated élites of Europe and North America began a long and tortuous investigation to understand these popular forms of culture so beloved by the masses but which seemed to violate every standard of decency, taste, and culture.[1]

In the 20th century this investigation became known as the *Mass Culture* debate and was thought to be responsible for everything from Fascism to child abuse by intellectuals despairing at what they saw as the demise of a centuries-old European civilisation. It was out of this *moral* debate about the significance of mass culture that analysts examined the social composition of the audiences so 'addicted' to the products of the new culture industry. They tried to determine who was consuming it, why were they so drawn to it and what were the features of mass culture that appeared to make it so attractive. This investigation of mass forms also turned its gaze upon the nature of the audiences for high culture.

The outcome of this was a reformulation of the differences between cultures into an horizontal band, rather than a vertical column made up of cultural forms of lessening quality; that is there was a move from a moral hierarchy to one where cultural differences were thought of in terms of an horizontal spread. This shift still causes enormous problems because it leaves the evaluative model of cultural differences in a great deal of trouble. For example, using an hierarchical evaluative model of Art and culture it seems obvious to regard the original *Mona Lisa* as being superior to the mass-produced imitation. The latter is garish, a simplification bereft of all the subtleties displayed by the original. And yet, if the two images are seen *within* the different groups they are important to, for example, the community of Art Historians and the Italian émigré groups, we are confronted with two different uses of the image, both of which are 'rational' when the values of the group in which they are in circulation is taken into account. The former sees the Mona Lisa as canonical to the European tradition of oil painting, the latter uses the many reproductions of it as an icon of national pride, as mnemonic denoting their origin within a major European civilisation.

The spread and domination of mass culture since the end of World War II means that today we are all cultural hybrids and all of us make up, to varying degrees, the audiences for mass culture. Today it is possible to visit Art museums *and* like rock music. Cultural and artistic forms that were previously tied to the exclusive ways of life of certain groups — the landed aristocracy or the high bourgeoisie — may now become possible options as one's status changes. The 'industralisation' of Art and culture has also lead to an increasing specialisation amongst audiences. Popular forms of rock music may begin to divide out into a series of styles consumed by particular subcultures: heavy metal, country and western, or avant-garde rock. A similar tendency appears to be happening within the tradition of classical music — romantic, easy listening classical favourites, avant-garde.

A situation is reached where the increasing specialisation of the Visual Arts begins to approximate to the situation music is now in. That is differing social groups or categories make different selections from the range of possibilities on offer. (A visit to shops specialising in cheap reproductions of 'masterpieces' of the European tradition will confirm how selective is the range of images which are for sale.) It is only possible to understand why particular choices are made by being cognisant of the internal logics and rationales that are guiding *that* social group's selections. It would follow that it is possible for whole social groups to be indifferent to, even antipathetical towards, Art forms that are considered by the educated ruling élites to be an essential acquisition of a cultured individual.

Difference in audiences

The astute reader will have realised that in our investigations of Box III a wide variety of terms have been used to denote what is taking place there. I want to attempt to sort out the similarities and differences between these various designations that have been utilised so far.

The term *subject* is the most general appellation and refers to 'the basic social unit of action, knowledge, and textual encounter', while the terms *viewer/spectator* are interchangeable but more restricted in their scope and refer to a 'subject who engages with the various ways of looking' at visual texts. The term *reader* is a double-faced entity. It indicates, firstly the 'position of implied/ model reader that a text projects and from which optimum sense may be made of that text', but it can also refer to the 'activities engaged in by the viewer/spectator', activities aimed at making sense of the encountered text.

The term *audience* carries within it an assumption of a 'collectivity' massed together to witness a cultural event, that is 'a group assembled together in one place all viewing a similar event/text'. Popular and mass cultural forms spring to mind here — music hall, sporting events, film, but there are also high cultural forms which have this mode of assembly — music and theatre.

Theories of the subject/viewer imply, even if they don't mean to, a situation where a single, isolated subject encounters the text such as reading a novel or looking at a work of Art. It is clear that both models can be transposed upon the contemporary situation. Cinema and television have a mass audience, the former relying upon a common assembly point, however the latter can be viewed in a more individualised situation. Likewise certain aspects of theories of the subject can be made relevant to the individual members of an audience — the 'reader' is clearly a concept that applies to all textual encounters whatever the particularities of the viewing situation. The term *audience* certainly retains notions of a common assembly point but in its modern formulation it is more likely to refer to the similarities *amongst* those consuming a particular cultural and artistic product.

Examine Figure 9.1.

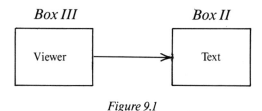

Figure 9.1

When we think of the term 'viewer' we will probably all call up in our minds a mental picture of someone standing in front of a work of Art. The word 'viewer' is an abstraction derived from concrete situations we have all been in. Once we start asking ourselves who is it who actually occupies that box then we must begin to ask questions about the different sorts of people who might walk into such a space.

The most vivid demonstration of the importance of paying heed to this is to visit your nearest art gallery and position yourself close to one of the 'celebrity' works. In the space of fifteen to thirty minutes one cannot help being struck by the *diversity* of viewers constituting the audience for a work. Given such diversity one cannot help asking what sense, or senses, are these people making of it? The real problem that this poses is, faced with an apparently unending succession of individuals, are we to proclaim that every encounter is different? We don't do this because while we are registering the differences we have seen *between* those examining the picture we are also slotting them *into* very broad social categories. That is we are also registering similarities.

We have already spoken about how texts project a place from which to comprehend them — that place we have referred to as the implied or model reader. But what happens if we approach this area from the other end? What factors might be operating in terms of the encounter between the *actual reader* and the text?

Examine illustration 43.

The model reader for this English seaside postcard is male and the point of the joke is a male viewer, but the butt of the joke is the woman represented in the image. The image works by engaging with two levels of punning — the linguistic heading 'They're off!' refers at one level to the start of the horserace but at another to the unfortunate accident that has befallen the woman. The joke is probably capable of causing hilarity in both male and female viewers, but the position we are put in in relation to the scene is that of the male viewer. The situation is one where the implicit/ model reader is male together with an *actual reader* who may be female. (We might also add that there is the assumption that the readers of this image are drawn from that particular group within the English class system which delights in the pleasures of bawdy puns.) Who one identifies within this image may certainly lessen the jocularity which the viewer experiences, although it may not overturn the force of the pun.

We may say, therefore, that what *the actual viewer* brings to the text in terms of their membership of a social group(s) or category(ies) is crucial for shaping the senses that are made of texts.

Race, class, gender, and place

The social make up of individuals is usually thought of in terms of four broad categories. These are the dimensions of gender, race, class, and place. (This last category is often formulated in terms of *nation*.) Once this is grasped it is possible to make a number of additions to Figure 9.1 (p. 187).

The disembodied eye of the abstract viewer/subject can now be placed within *a social field* consisting of the four social categories.

But, as in all of our considerations of the viewer, we must also consider the text. The categories of gender, race, class, and place also impinge but here they appear within the visual text but in a coded form (*see* illustration 44). This image is taken from a children's book produced during the Nazi rule of Germany in the 1930s. I have chosen this repulsive and extreme example because it

43. Donald McGill: English seaside postcard

highlights the factor of coding in a particularly sharp way. In this instance it is racial coding — to the left are three Jewish men represented in stereotypical fashion, whilst to their right three black crows — a symbol for the black races in general — can be

44. Nazi children's book illustration, 1930s
(The Institute of Contemporary History and Wiener Library Ltd, London)

seen. (In the Nazi world view the blacks were regarded as the un-witting agents of the Jewish conspiracy against the blonde haired, blue-eyed Aryan nations.)

It follows that we must also make some additions to the textual pole of Figure 9.2.

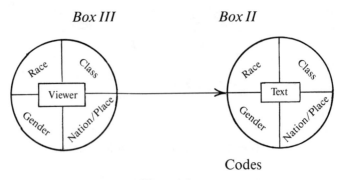

Figure 9.2

Both *viewer and text* must now be seen as points embedded within a network of social relations. The viewer can be 'fleshed out' in terms of their placement within the social categories whilst the visual text can be thought of as an area where these social categories may appear in a coded form.

I want to make a number of general observations about these social categories, particularly how they may be used and abused in the analyses of audiences and works of Art before looking at them in greater detail.

We *all* belong to *all* of the social categories, but we experience them individually. This is important because when we use such broad social categories it is easy to flatten out and homogenise the texture of an individual biography as well as the multiple dimensions of a particular text. Gender, race, class, and place are forces that unify us *into* audiences at the same time as differentiating us from one another.

It is necessary always to consider these categories *together*; if just one is selected and stressed at the expense of the others an impoverishment of our readings will occur. In the example of the McGill postcard it was gender that was initially picked out, but class is also important because the form of the joke, a risqué pun, was a type of humour much appreciated by both *men and women* of certain sections of the English working class. We might say that audiences and texts might be thought of as musical notes which are struck when these categories are deployed. To simply trace, for instance, the melody of class, without taking into account the accompanying harmonics and counterpoint destroys the complexities of the encounter.

Each of these categories cannot be thought of in isolation. They all carry within them assumptions about power relationships, that is they tend to concern themselves with the relative positions between their implied viewer and the figures depicted. Class implies relations *between* classes, or the coding of differences. Gender carries the idea of the relations *between* men and women and the coding of their differences. Race/ethnicity is concerned with differences *between* human and cultural groups and this is usually conducted in terms of evaluative comparisons. Place/ nation implies both membership within a community as well as the relations and differences between that nation and others. Finally, one cannot determine *a priori* what particular social category will weigh most heavily in any particular situation. In certain circumstances class may be the most powerful factor, whilst in others nationality may be the most important.

The social category that is in dominance — for instance nationality — may be able to create a unity in the audience and its reading of a particular visual text by repressing or excluding the dimensions of race, class, and gender.

Culture and biology

I have listed the social categories in the order of gender, race, class, and place/nation because as we move across these categories it should be possible to see how each one of them is differentially placed into the domain of biology or nature. That is each social category searches for an explanation of itself within the 'facts' of human biology or the 'natural order'. So gender appears to describe differences deriving from the anatomical variation between males and females. Race would appear to describe differences deriving from the anatomical and physical varieties within the species *homo sapiens*. Class and nation are, these days, less heavily biologised although there are still remnants of an earlier biologism. Class differences can be discussed in terms of distinctive physical and mental traits, nationality certainly likes to think it is capable of pinpointing distinctive 'ways of life' which slip over into assertions about national psychologies and identities.

I am not saying that biological and physical variety and difference does not exist but here I am concerned with the sense that is made of these differences by culture and society. Rather than reducing differences between individuals to biology and nature, my aim here is to see how it is that biology becomes a set of social meanings, how it is *coded* into meaning.

Gender

The first distinction to be made here is that between *a person's sex* — their anatomical 'equipment' derived from their genetic inheritance — and *a person's gender* — that is the sense or meaning which is made of sex by a particular society. There are always going to be male and female sexes but the meaning or significance of the male and female sex will vary with time and place. Sex refers to the anatomical structure, gender refers to the social significance which is made of the anatomical differences.

This collective meaning of 'gender' has relevance for the visual text and the viewer. In terms of the *text* it means that gender is always a *coded area*. Gender, both within and without the visual image is always a matter of encountering the *signs* of gender; one might even say that gender *is* a sign of masculinity and femininity. This is not to say that an image simply reproduces within its space external codes of gender, rather that the edge or the frame that we have talked about so much constitutes a coding threshold — cross that line and a particular set of ways of *coding gender* becomes permissible. We can see this at its most intense with images that represent *idealised* representations of the male and female (*see* ills 45, 46). In each of these examples what is happening is that the images are utilising the codes for *the depiction* of the male and female; the ways in which they are permitted to appear within the frame.

At the audience/viewer pole the move is from biological sex to a gendered position within culture, but here it is the individual human animal that is at stake. Currently there are two main theoretical models which have attempted to explain how sex and gender interlock; how sex is transformed into gender. These are *the psycho-analytic* and the *social learning theory.*

Psycho-analytical theory is dominated by the work of Sigmund Freud who stated that it was the aim of psycho-analysis to explore: 'Some psychical (mental) consequences of the anatomical distinction between the sexes.' Psycho-analysis, then, has two aims:

(a) To explain, how in the human species, the journey is made from animal to human, from nature to culture, from sex to gender and what are the consequences (to us) of having to make such a journey.

(b) An investigation of how it is that the two anatomies (male and female) generate different psychical experiences/realities. It should be noted that difference here refers not to two separate and distinct entities, but differences in relation to one another. Being of the male gender also means not being female and vice versa.

Despite the controversy which still surrounds the work of Freud and his followers, it has firmly established that entry into the adult social world entails entry into a psychic structure which rests upon the individual 'accepting' with varying degrees of compliance, the social sense that is made of anatomical genital differences.

Social learning theory differs from psycho-analysis. It claims to be able to describe how gender arises by explaining how gender is *learnt* and functions within society. Rather than emphasising — as does psycho-analysis — what it is like to be *inside* gender (what it is like to be a man or a woman), social learning theory concen-

45. Hilda Rix Nicholas: *A man* 1921. Oil on canvas, 92 x 75 cm.
(Australian War Memorial [19613])

trates upon gender as a set of *learned responses*. Gender exists and
continues to operate because individuals are *taught* to be men and
women. Gender, in this model, is essentially a distinctive way *of
acting* in the world.

These two models have added considerably to the way we think
about gender. Gender can be the acquired knowledge of what a
pre-given anatomy means within a particular society. Acquisition
of one's gender means the acquisition of a particular way of being,

46. Albert Varga: Varga Girl *Esquire Magazine* 1944.
(Spencer Museum of Art, University of Kansas)

feeling and acting in the world. It means being placed within (or rejecting and rebelling against) *a number of codes* which define what it is to be masculine or feminine.

Race
Like gender, ideas about race may rest upon an underlying substratum of physical difference and human variety, but it is the sense that is made of these variations and meanings that they acquire which is crucial. The social categories of race (and gender) are not simply 'reflectors' of actual differences, they can be powerful labelling devices which take on the force of reality.

    Race, rather than being an absolute pre-given, is something which is made within the world of culture and we can see how social and cultural factors become active agents in its formation in the shift that occurs from talking about *race* to speaking about *ethnicity*. In the former there may, in fact, be a set of physical differences but as we move towards ethnicity (which is largely about *cultural differences*) spurious physical 'motives' may still be called upon to explain cultural differences.

Each of the social categories we are dealing with here automatically brings considerations of power into play. That is they are involved in ideas about the ways in which social groups organise power relations, either internally between members of differing social categories, or externally in the relations of dominance and subordination they establish with other groups. For instance, in considerations of gender relations of power exist between men and women, likewise with race ideas of superiority/inferiority are inescapable. We might say that race does not exist in any descriptively meaningful way and cannot explain any important event in history. But *racism* does and has existed, and it is racism, in the sense of culturally constructed ideas about inferiority/superiority, that enables us to understand such events.

It is important to stress that race and racism are not simply 'things' that can be read off an image in terms of *how* an artist has depicted the physical characteristics of people from different racial or ethnic groups to that of the depicter. Racism always involves *more* than a stereotyping of their physical appearance in that representations of other groups will be embedded in complex systems of coding through which and with which one culture is able to imagine and depict other cultures and other peoples. Such systems of coding are very often concerned with the *relationships between* the two cultures — that of the depicter and that of the depicted. I stress this point because it is rarely the case that the truth of such representations can be determined by appealing to a real or accurate set of characteristics which is then deliberately 'distorted' by the artist in question. Such accurate knowledge is frequently absent and anyway such images are rarely about these peoples in themselves, but are about where the depicting culture imagines them to be in relation to the 'home' culture. Race and racism then is concerned with a set of wishes, anxieties even fantasies about where and what this other entity is. From the viewpoint of Europe, other peoples have been depicted in many ways. For instance, in the 18th century, Europeans depicted the peoples of the South Pacific as 'noble savages'. In the 19th century the East was thought of as a continent in the grip of tyranny and languid sensualism, whilst the Africans have been consistently depicted by Europeans as 'primitives', with all the connotations of instinctual, and non-civilised that this word brings.

So racism need not necessarily be derogatory towards the other (although it often is), but can code a people to become an ideal to be aspired towards — a desirable utopia. It can be the inverse of the home society — an antipodes, or the repressed underside of an overcivilised way of life — the primitive. In each case it is the relationship between two entities (real or imagined) that is the essence of the visual codings.

Class

It is generally agreed that class exists but getting a consensus about what it consists of, and how it operates in visual imagery is much more difficult. The following general points should be borne in mind:

- It is involved with, and attempts to describe, the internal, hierarchical divisions that exist within any given society
- It is something to do with the positioning of social groups in the overall *economic* structure of a society
- It is as much about the culture, the way of life of these groups, as it is about the economic position of each group
- It involves differential access to power (particularly political power) and therefore brings into play very complex relations of domination and subordination between class groups

Which of the factors listed above one wishes to stress will depend upon where one places oneself within the political spectrum. Every modern complex society has a class system but each society has a different class structure (pattern of relations between classes) which is the product of each nation's differential history and experience.

If we now pose the question 'how does class impinge upon the reading of visual images', it should already be clear that some of the mechanisms we have been describing in relation to gender and race will be re-encountered in the area of class. According to the nature of the particular class structure we are dealing with, there may be varying degrees of *difference* between the cultures associated with particular class groups. For instance 19th-century and 20th century class structures in western Europe displayed a marked difference between the culture of the middle classes and that of the working class. It should be clear that the Art that is the major focus of this book cannot under any circumstances be described as working class culture. Like race, class relations also rest upon notions of superiority and inferiority and it is common to find that the Art and culture of one class may be regarded as superior to that of another. We have already noted that during the 19th and 20th centuries the middle classes of Europe regarded the culture of the lower classes as dangerous and threatening.

The Art and culture of the dominant class can be the basis for generalised systems of taste, that is systems for evaluating and discriminating between the acceptable and the impoverished. For instance during the 1950s and early 1960s in the UK I had to study Latin for six years. Without a certificate in this subject entry to many English universities to study the subjects I was interested in would have been barred to me. The compulsory status of Latin derived from 18th-century and 19th-century ideas about what an educated/cultivated individual should learn, which in turn rested upon the European aristocracy's admiration of Classical learning.

Because artistic codes of visual depiction are frequently the property of the powerful élites within any society — the upper classes, the Church or the State — the 'lower orders' have often found themselves being coded visually in terms of an 'other' or different to those owning such codes. These differences have a long and complex history in Europe. For instance, in the 19th-century European Romantic artists depicted peasants and rural workers as embodying all the virtues of an organic and traditional way of life. These were often contrasted with the urban proletariat which had undergone a systematic degradation and brutalisation with the onset of the industrial system of production. Victorian artists, disturbed by the emergence of an 'other' in the form of an organised working class, vacillated between presenting them as either simple and honest or dangerous and libidinal. In the 20th century the Stalinist regime in the Soviet Union heroicised and romanticised the worker in the style of Art known as Socialist Realism.

If we consider class from the perspective of appreciating works of Art in general, we find that there is a differential distribution of what we may term the 'codes of reading'. Many people not in possession of such codes may be unable or unwilling to adopt the position of the co-operative reader. This may manifest itself in terms of a widespread indifference or antipathy towards forms of Art that might be termed 'high' or 'avant-garde'.

Nationality/Place

In the 19th and 20th centuries, along with gender, race, and class, nationality has been an important factor in determining who and what people imagine they are. In fact, at various moments questions of nationality and its associated emotion of patriotism have been extremely powerful in welding together disparate groups and social categories. In Europe, nationalism has been the cause of numerous wars but since the end of World War II the presence of an external 'threat' in the form of the USSR has been instrumental in lessening the emphasis upon the nation. But in areas of the world where other political and social circumstances prevail many countries have used nationalism as a way of creating a distinct identity for their peoples. Not all of these reasons for nationalism have been successful. Divisions based upon tribal, ethnic and racial differences have persisted and often been the cause of bloody conflicts. Again, what is crucial in these emerging nations is the creation of a specific national culture, that is a set of signs, symbols, and stories, which speak of a common experience, something that will point to a unity within, but also will mark the nation off as being different to other such groupings. This process of constructing a national communality and difference may utilise cultural elements whose task is to erase cultural memories deriving from earlier and perhaps more divisive ways of life. In the context of Australia, paintings produced in the 1890s and early 1900s have come to be seen as *the* moment when a distinctively Antipodean style of painting came into being.[2] The work of the painters of the Heidelberg School (Charles Conder, Tom Roberts, Arthur Streeton, and Frederick McCubbin to name several) and their appropriation of French Impressionist techniques can be interpreted as an attempt on the part of such painters to produce work that did justice to the Australian land-scape and the distinctive features of the light, vegetation, and sentiments felt towards it. This they did without utilising English models. In this sense it was both 'Australian' and anti-colonial.

Two Readings

Having discussed the social categories in terms of their more general relations to Art and culture I want to bring this chapter (and the book) to a close by examining two images in the light of gender, race, class, and nation.

We will begin with the photograph (ill. 47). I first encountered this photograph whilst browsing through a book about cities in

19th-century Britain. At first it set up nothing more than a ripple as I was turning the pages, but this was enough to send me back to it time and again to discover what it was that had disturbed me.

The caption accompanying the photograph read as follows, 'A tipster at Aintree, 1901. Decked in the rags of Empire.' I finally realised that what was intriguing me was the conjunction of the date, the place, and the black figure. Why was this? What the picture revealed to me was that there was a *black Englishman* in a northern city at the time. This fact intersected with my past — as a white Englishman, born in 1944 who had grown up in a country where I had imagined that black migration to England started during the 1950s and 1960s from the Caribbean. Before that my only encounters with black people had been through signs.

Every Christmas as a child, I had looked forward to being given a box of sweet ginger largely because on the label was depicted a black servant, dressed in a 'flunkey's' uniform (a blackamoor) and carrying an exotic Chinese ginger jar. This depiction was a remnant of the 18th century when blacks were favoured as servants by the upper class. As far as I was concerned blacks were Africans, people who had been conquered by the British. They were exotic figures who appeared in children's books and comics where they were always dressed in leopard skins and spoke gibberish. What had happened when I encountered the image of the tipster was that I was suddenly made aware of a black presence in the United Kingdom which had been erased, or rather had never surfaced, in my childhood imagination.

Looking at the image a number of things began to fall in place. The fact that the anonymous photographer had decided that this man was worthy of photographing signalled to me that a black man was regarded at the time as something of an anomaly, something special and different from the everyday scenes he might have captured with his camera. This is confirmed by the two white figures placed on the extreme left and right of the frame who seem torn between an interest in the act of photographing itself and the black. Both are objects of curiosity and intrigue. The black looks away and down from the camera as if being photographed is intrusive and threatening. Keeping ones eyes averted from the gaze of those in power is a common stance of the ruled.

A simple piece of research revealed that there had been a considerable black presence in Great Britain for almost 200 years before this photograph was taken. They had been concentrated in

47. A black tipster at Aintree, England, 1901
(Courtesy Liverpool Public Library)

the major ports of the country — Bristol, Cardiff, Liverpool, and
London — the first three locations notorious as slaving centres
until its abolition in the early part of the 19th century. However,
their percolation to other areas of the country had always been
limited and they had formed small, inward-looking communities

marginal to even the white working classes which dominated these cities. So for at least 250 years they had existed inside of a double alienation, neither 'natives' nor fully paid-up members of English society, albeit in a very lowly position.

That the black man was a tipster was no coincidence. A tipster was someone who sold his/her knowledge of possible winners of horseraces to the uninformed punters. As the taking of money in the form of bets was illegal this service was a quasi-legal way of earning a living from the races. Such an individual would be drawn to the race track because it was one of the areas where the strict social apartheid between the classes was slackened as they mixed together momentarily in the pursuit of gambling. (Jockeys, trainers, and racing fraternity were always of a very different class from the racehorse owners.) At a race meeting many individuals would buy tips and it was important that the tipsters were able to draw attention to themselves as being *different* in order to attract potential customers. The black tipster has attempted to do this by a double strategy — one that draws attention to his difference, his blackness, his exotic nature, the other by displaying signs of belonging. It would be one occasion where his black skin could work for him, but at the same time he displays, in his bizzare costume 'the rags of Empire'. On his feet are clogs, the traditional footwear of working class cotton millworkers. Alongside of this 'civilian' form of footwear he has assembled a veritable archive of British military costumes. On his head he wears the sun helmet of the British Army, probably a remnant from the Boer War in which the British had secured their hold over southern Africa. He has two military greatcoats — probably a sign he was sleeping rough — on which are sewn military stripes. On the front are attached a motley collection of military medals and stripes. Across his shoulder he carries the bag in which he keeps his pieces of paper upon which are written his racing tips: this costume is a parody of the English soldier, of those class attitudes where the fiercest patriots are not the rich, but the working class who fervently believe that the supreme virtue for an Englishman is to die fighting for his country on some foreign shore.

This reading is neither a purely personal one (completely dependent upon my own history) nor is it an interpretation which aims to determine the meaning of this image independent of my history. Its significance derives from what happened *after* it had been taken. The 'ripple' was a tiny deposit left behind by the subsequent unfolding of black/white relations inside the UK. The reading arises precisely because it is generated by my particular social composition in terms of race and nation and the way this intersects with the information presented to me by the image. Rather than thinking of the codes of race, gender, class, and nation as being permanently fixed in the viewer and the image one must think of them as *differentially circulating* through these points. For instance, contemporary black Englishmen encountering such an image may produce a set of very different readings. They may point to the fact that black people were marginalised in 1901 as evidence of the continuing racism of white society that still sees these people as exotic, different or 'not English'. They may see the costume of the black tipster as poignant, evidence of the 'Uncle Tom' psychology of earlier black people who were afraid of asserting a legitimate identity for themselves as *black Englishmen*. My final point is that the life experiences of the viewer cannot be artificially excluded from one's reading of the image. These are part of the luggage we *all* bring to our encounters with visual images precisely because both images and their readers sit within such social categories.

Look at the illustration of Picasso's *Les Demoiselles d'Avignon* (ill. 48). Those even slightly familiar with the story of Modern Art know the central place accorded to this painting. Even before we begin to consider what is taking place in this image it will already have a meaning, namely that it is an 'important' painting for the history of Modernism. 'This is where it all began.'

This strange and violent image moves in a number of directions. It is well known that the artist studied a number of African masks in order to infuse the image with a feeling of, and for, the primitive. But we need to ask what did *primitivism* mean in the formative years of Modernism? Certainly it enabled a number of artists to avail themselves of a set of non-European plastic strategies — distortion, simplification, and grotesqueness. But primitivism always meant something more than a set of fresh visual devices. The primitive meant 'instinctual', it meant 'unbounded spontaneity', and line freed from rational or mimetic considerations. It was a way for certain artists to 'go native' in their work. But this 'going native' was not an attempt to do as the Africans did, but to do and be what these artists *imagined* Africans were. Primitivism in this period of early Modernism involved a very particular form of making sense of these non-European artifacts, and in this the

48. Pablo Picasso: *Les Demoiselles d'Avignon* 1907. Oil on canvas, 243.9 x 233.7 cm (Collection, The Museum of Modern Art, New York)

African masks were always more than a novel artistic resource through which the formal properties of the image could be re-imagined.

This image was painted at a time (1907) when France had, and still was, acquiring a vast African empire and when European Imperialism was reaching its apogee. The white countries thought of themselves as the bearers of civilisation and reason. They were the future of the world. This meant that there were in circulation a set of very powerful ideas about the relations between white, European civilisation and black, African civilisations. It is clear that by utilising such non-European artifacts in the way that they did these artists were launching a criticism of certain aspects of European civilisation. In such paintings it was the instinctual that was stressed over the rational, the spontaneous rather than the controlled. Any powerful emotion, no matter how violent, was better than the bland emotional range of much European Art of the time. However, this was not therefore a championing of the rights of colonial subjects overseas, rather the erection of a fantasy alternative which drew upon elements of African Art to facilitate the dream of violent renewal.

Picasso was a Spaniard and a Catalan and it is known that as well as drawing upon artifacts from the colonies of France, he also went back in time to study objects from his own regional and national past. This past was drawn into his present, but it was a regional past that had existed before the implantation of European civilisation in Spain. In order to make the new, Picasso made the double move of far away and long ago.

What is crucial in all of this cultural ransacking is that the dimensions we have detailed above — the archaic, the primitive, the instinctual, the terrifying — all collide in the figures of the women in the painting, and now questions about gender need to be raised.

The women in the image are in classical poses derived from the tradition of European sculpture and painting. In these figures the artist has clearly set out to both desecrate and travesty these traditional codes for depicting the female form. But why is the figure of the woman made the vehicle of this desecratory urge?

It is here that the earlier codes of primitivism intersect with those of gender. In this painting it is European women who become the place where the primitive can be detected at home. Women are different, the other of men in that they are more like the African and the ancient Catalans than they are European men. It is they who represent the archaic and primitive within this image.

It is as if two powerful emotions — attraction and repulsion — were being made to co-exist within the same image. Women and the primitive are both desirable and terrifying and it is this set of ambiguities that to my mind constitute its nightmarish savagery.[3]

Having said this, it is worth pointing out that a reading such as I've conducted has only been made possible by a series of events that have taken place after the production of the image. It is a reading that could only be undertaken after the impact of the Women's Movement and the de-colonisation of the European land Empires.

These two readings should enable you to see how the social categories under discussion can throw light upon images and the ways viewers approach them. However prestigious the artist making the marks may be, however daunting the thought of taking up a critical position towards the famous may appear, it should always be remembered that they are undertaking the act of production from *somewhere*. This is not to say that we simply read off race, gender, class, or nation as an automatic checklist and let out with a cry of foul or bias! It may even be that these social categories are not always the most relevant issues in and around a particular work of Art. Rather the categories race, gender, class, and nation are factors which both flow through images and through us as we encounter them. As such they are factors which can enrich our readings, not invalidate them.

1   The standard work on this debate is Raymond Williams *Culture and Society: 1780-1950* London: Pelican, 1961.
2   *See* Bernard Smith *Australian Painting: 1788-1960* Melbourne: 1971.
3   I am indebted to Charles Merewether for this reading of the *Demoiselles.*

Index

References made to endnotes have *n.* preceding the number;
illustration references are in bold.

Also available in this series:

Illusions of Identity: The Art of Nation
by Anne-Marie Willis 208 pp.
$22.95 paperback 0 86806 357 6

This book aims to go beyond the familiar approach of studying the art of a particular nation as an 'expression' of assumed characteristics of that nation. So instead of asking 'what is distinctive about Australian art?', it looks at how visual imagery works to construct versions of national identity.

Topics include conquering/picturing the land; images of racism; modernity and modernism; imagery of war; and the nation as brand name.

Old Worlds, New Visions
by Tony Fry 160 pp.
$19.95 paperback 0 86806 353 3; $35.00 hardback 0 86806 352 5

This presents new frameworks for understanding Modernity, Modernism, and visual cultures in the twentieth century. It presents multiple perspectives for a range of visual objects found not only in the spaces of institutions but in the everyday world. Using five case studies, the book fleshes out the theories under discussion in a challenging and readily comprehensible manner. Cases include a painting (Delaunay's Eiffel Tower); a building (the Larking Building); a design object (the Sydney Harbour Bridge); a mural (Oswaldo Guayasamin's 'History of the Civilisation'); and a photograph ('Lady with a Lamp').

Also available from Hale & Iremonger:

The Critical Distance
edited by Virginia Coventry 200 pp.
$35.00 hardback 0 86806 223 5

Lavishly illustrated with over 240 photographs in colour and black and white, this book is a collection of essays, statements and work by 14 contemporary Australian photographers, which reflect the social, political and aesthetic concerns of recent years. Contributors include Mickey Allan, Ruth Maddison, Peter Lyssiotis, and Toni Robertson.

Design History Australia
by Tony Fry 172 pp.
$19.95 paperback 0 86806 322 3;
$35.00 hardback 0 86806 321 5

Design history is a relatively neglected area of study in Australia and section one of this book presents a much needed critical overview of the subject. Section two proposes an approach to design appropriate to Australia. Section three applies this method to three case studies, and section four contains a comprehensive listing of sources.

Painters in the Australian Landscape
by Robert Walker 172 pp.
$35 paperback 0 86806 339 8

Superbly illustrated in full colour throughout, **Painters in the Australian Landscape** presents a series of photographic impressions, together with conversations and reproductions of paintings, that examine the lives and environment of fourteen noted Australian artists.

The book features the work of John Olsen, Charles Blackman, Robert Juniper, Clifton Pugh, Brett Whiteley, Tim Storrier, Arthur Boyd, Ray Crooke, Keith Looby, Lawrence Dawes, John Firth-Smith, Frank Hodgkinson, Wendy Stavrianos and John Wolseley.